GUITAR SCALES 365

BY KIRK TATNA

MW00892304

ISBN: 9798345124536

HOW TO GET THE AUDIO

The audio files for this book are available for free as downloads or streaming on *troynelsonmusic.com*.

We are available to help you with your audio downloads and any other questions you may have. Simply email *help@troynelsonmusic.com*.

See below for the recommended ways to listen to the audio:

Download Audio Files	Stream Audio Files
• Download Audio Files (Zipped)	• Recommended for CELL PHONES & TABLETS
• Recommended for COMPUTERS on WiFi	• Bookmark this page
• A ZIP file will automatically download to the default "downloads" folder on your computer	• Simply tap the PLAY button on the track you want to listen to
• Recommended: download to a desktop/laptop computer *first*, then transfer to a tablet or cell phone	• Files also available for streaming or download at *soundcloud.com/troynelsonbooks*
• Phones & tablets may need an "unzipping" app such as iZip, Unrar or Winzip	
• Download on WiFi for faster download speeds	

To download the companion audio files for this book, visit: troynelsonmusic.com/audio-downloads/

INTRODUCTION

Welcome to *Guitar Scales 365*. The goal of this book is to provide a clear path to learning the essential scale patterns needed to make music, one day at a time. With just a few minutes of daily practice, you will unlock the fretboard and be able to use these scales in all 12 keys.

WHAT IS A SCALE?

As defined by *Merriam-Webster*, a scale is "a graduated series of musical tones ascending or descending in order of pitch according to a specified scheme of their intervals." More simply, you might think of a scale as being a musical alphabet of notes that songs are composed from, or a group of notes that will fit a song or chord progression for improvising. The sound of a scale is defined by how far apart each note is from the next.

WHOLE AND HALF STEPS

Half steps and *whole steps* are terms used to measure the distance between notes. A *half step* (H) is the smallest distance you can move; it's equivalent to moving up or down one key at a time on the piano, or one fret at a time on the guitar. A *whole step* (W) is equal to two half steps and is equivalent to moving two keys on the piano or two frets on the guitar. Since the distance between notes defines a scale, they are often represented this way: W W H W W W H. When the need for three half steps occurs, we will use W+H throughout the book.

READING SCALE DIAGRAMS

Scale diagrams are used to visually represent the guitar fretboard and show how scale patterns fit on it. The strings run horizontally, with the 6th string on the bottom of the diagram, and the 1st string at the top. You'll notice that string 6 is thicker than string 1 in the diagram, just like your guitar. The vertical lines represent frets. Use the fret numbers below the diagram and the grey fretboard dots to move the diagram to the correct location along the fretboard. The white dots represent the root note (1st note and name of the scale), and black dots represent all others. Inside each dot will be either a finger number or a note name.

A MAJOR PENTATONIC – FINGERINGS

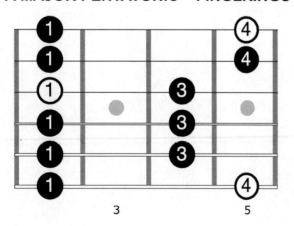

C MAJOR PENTATONIC – NOTE NAMES

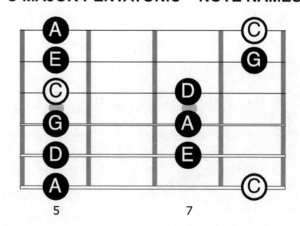

READING GUITAR TABLATURE

In addition to standard notation, this book uses a numeric notation system called *tablature*, or *tab*. In tab, the six horizontal lines represent the six strings of the guitar. The top line is your 1st string, and the bottom line is your 6th string. The numbers placed on the lines indicate the fret on which the note should be played. For example, a "5" placed on the top line indicates that you play string 1, fret 5. An "8" on the bottom line indicates that you play string 6, fret 8. Open strings are indicated with a "0." For example, when placed on the 3rd line from the top, a "0" would mean that you play your 3rd (G) string open (with no fingers).

THE CAGED SYSTEM

Using the shapes of our basic open chords, the CAGED system provides a way to map out the guitar fretboard and transpose these chords to any key. The chords provide landmarks for mapping out the scale patterns that surround them. In addition to providing a great acronym, CAGED represents how each shape connects to another along the fretboard. Study the diagrams below. Each row begins with the open chord, how it is turned into a moveable chord shape, and where the chord is located within the scale (white dots = chord tones).

Each open chord shape below is transposed to the key of A, since A major occurs first in our book. If this concept is difficult to grasp at first, don't worry—that's natural. The main takeaway is to associate the chord shape with the scale pattern.

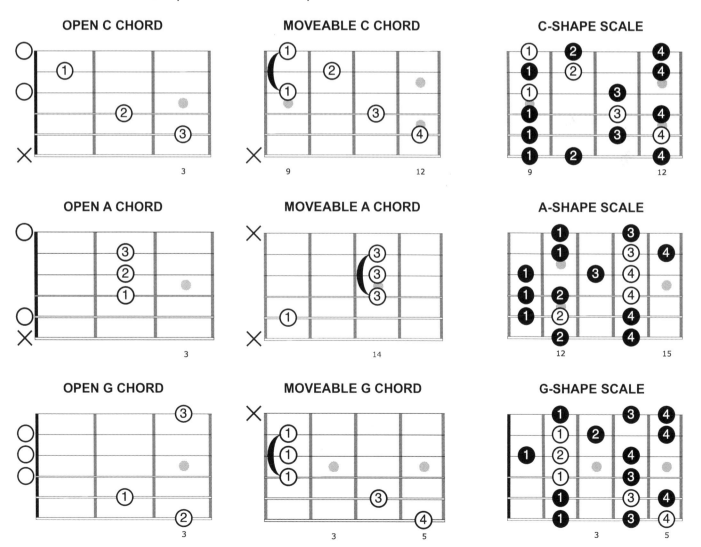

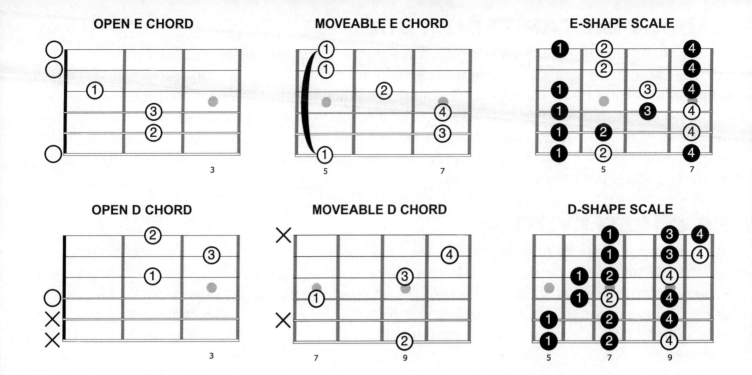

As mentioned previously, CAGED is actually the order in which these chords and scale patterns connect to each other along the fretboard via a shared note. The C Shape connects to the A Shape on the 5th string. The A Shape connects to the G shape on the 3rd string. The G Shape connects to the E Shape on the 6th string. The E Shape connects to the D shape on the 4th string. And, finally, the D Shape connects back to the C Shape on the 2nd string. Depending on what key you're in, the shape you start on as you go through the book will change according to which pattern is lowest on the fretboard, but it will always cycle through the word CAGED. Study the following diagrams.

CAGED CHORDS: KEY OF C MAJOR

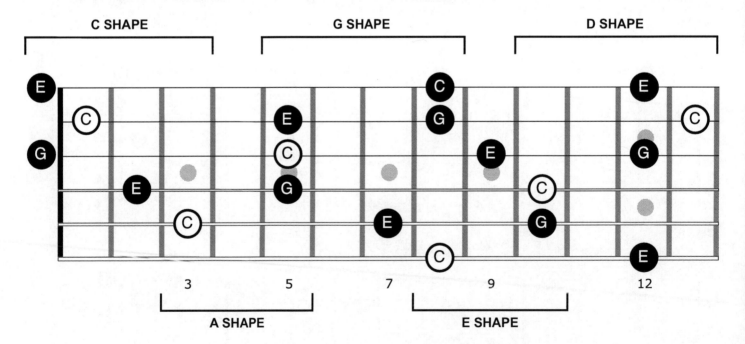

CAGED CHORDS: KEY OF A MAJOR

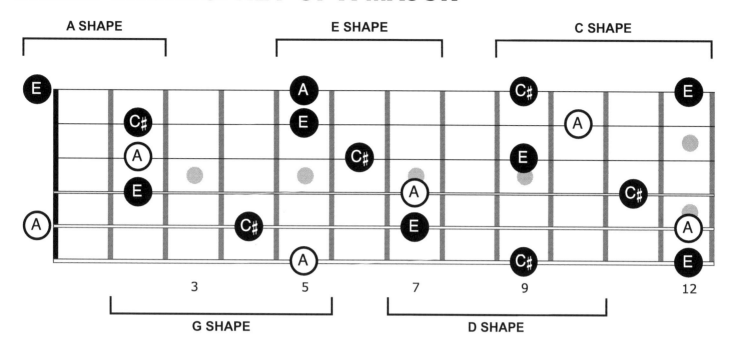

When using the CAGED system with minor chords, you'll find that the chords and scales connect in the same fashion: the white dots indicate the location of the root note and where the Shapes connect to each other. A *minor chord* is created by lowering the 3rd of the major chord by a half step (E to E♭ for C minor, and C♯ to C for A minor).

Minor scales are created by shifting the starting note of its relative major scale (the major scale sharing the same notes; for example, C major and A minor) to its 6th step. Since the minor scale is created by simply changing the starting note of its major counterpart, you'll find that the fingerings for these major and minor scales are identical. In other words, *the vast majority of this book involves mastering just five scale patterns* (the pentatonic scales are derived from these patterns, too!). Focus on "seeing the scale" between the root notes and refer back to these diagrams as needed.

CAGED CHORDS: KEY OF C MINOR

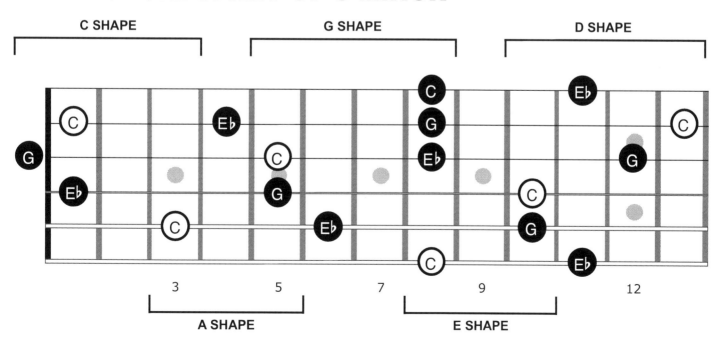

CAGED CHORDS: KEY OF A MINOR

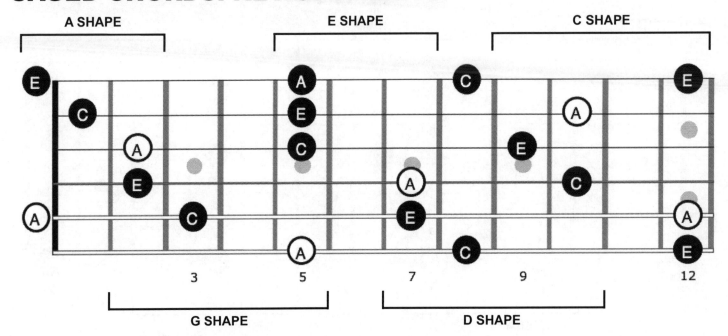

HOW TO USE THIS BOOK

The concept of this book is to have one small task to do every day. Doing so will cement the scale patterns into memory and enable you to recall and use them while making music. Simply follow these three steps:

1. **Strum the chord and play the scale as written.** Playing the chord will set up the sound of the scale while simultaneously creating an association with the scale pattern—almost like a monument within a city.

2. **Descend the scale.** Although the daily exercises are mostly written in ascending order, it's important to play them in both directions (use the scale diagrams for help). Make sure you end on the root (white dots) to ensure hearing the sound of the scale.

3. **Have fun with the scale pattern!** While ascending and descending scales for memorization is absolutely necessary, melodies involve much more variety, including skipping notes, changing direction, and varying rhythms. Throughout this book, Sundays will offer different ways to be musical with scales—and you can create your own, as well! A simple YouTube search of "G major backing track" or "C minor backing track" will yield many opportunities to use the scale pattern you're learning in a musical environment. Even going up and down a scale pattern with a backing track is fun and will help you absorb it.

PRACTICE TIPS

The most important aspect of this book is to play the scales daily. A small amount of daily practice is much better than two hours in one day and nothing the rest of the week! In fact, you can accomplish all three steps in 5–10 minutes of practice. As you're first learning the scales, they will naturally be more difficult, but by the time you've made it through a couple of keys, the fingerings will become familiar. Don't fret over memorizing the patterns—this will happen naturally as you continue to cycle through new keys.

WEEK 1: A MAJOR

The *major scale* is the most important scale to learn, as many other scales originate from it. Before we learn our first pattern, let's examine how it's constructed.

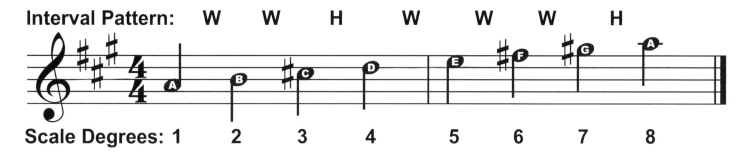

MONDAY: G SHAPE 1

Remember to use the 3-step method from "How to Use This Book." You can also refer to the chord pictures in the CAGED section when necessary.

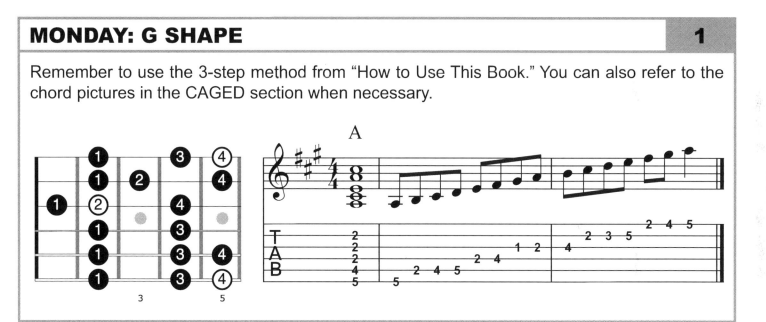

TUESDAY: E SHAPE 2

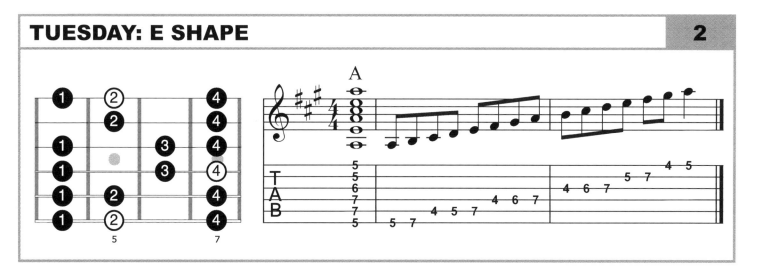

WEDNESDAY: D SHAPE

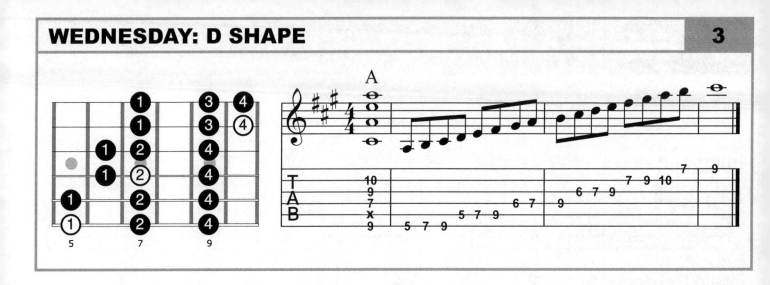

THURSDAY: C SHAPE

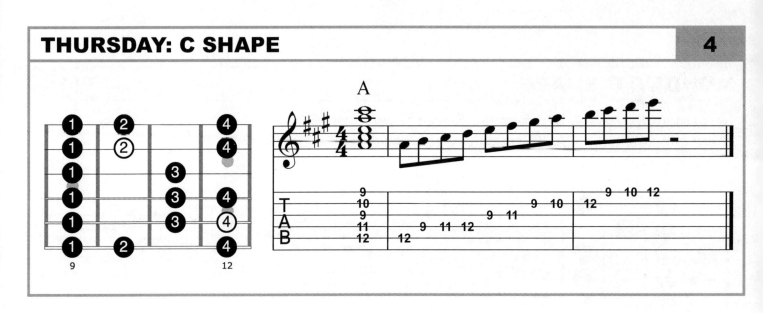

FRIDAY: A SHAPE

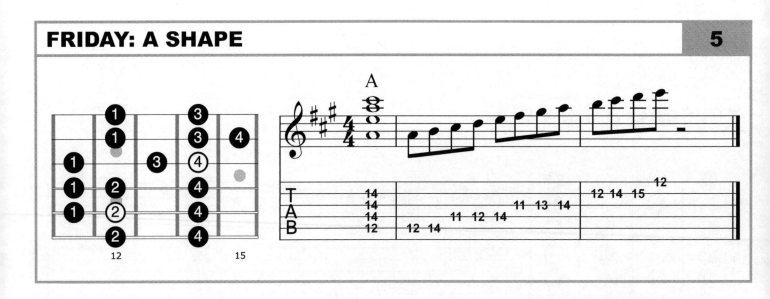

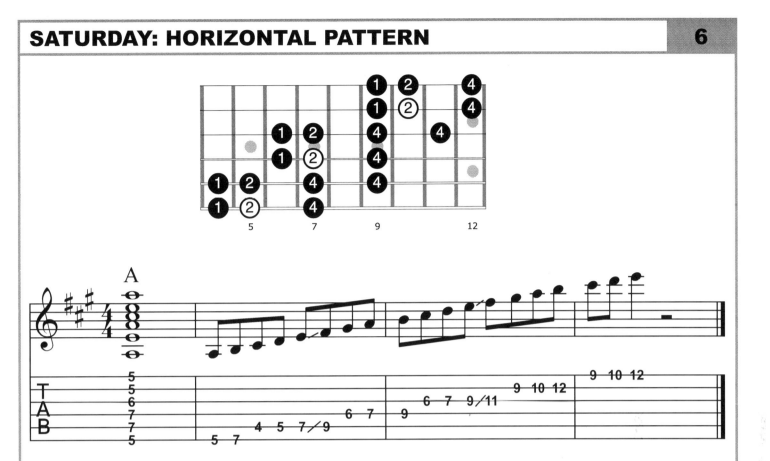

Moving from one note of a scale to the next, without skipping any notes, is referred to as "stepwise motion." Melodies often change direction within a small group of notes moving stepwise. Adding a rhythm results in excitement, motion, and an element of repetition to build an idea and draw in the listener. The melody below uses the E-Shape A major scale. Before you play it, listen to the audio while counting "1, 2-and, (3), 4". After learning this one, try making up your own!

WEEK 2: A MINOR

The *natural minor scale* is created by shifting the starting note (root) of its relative major scale to the 6th degree (C to A in the case of C major/A minor). Let's examine its interval pattern (the flatted 3rd, 6th, and 7th are the alterations required to turn A major into A minor).

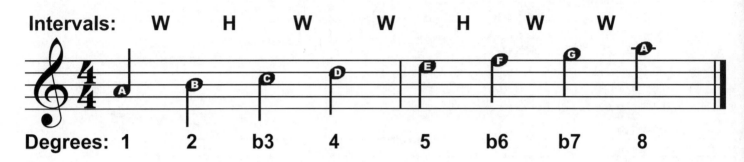

Intervals:	W	H	W	W	H	W	W
Degrees: 1	2	b3	4	5	b6	b7	8

MONDAY: G SHAPE 8

Don't forget to use the 3-step method from "How to Use This Book" (page 8)!

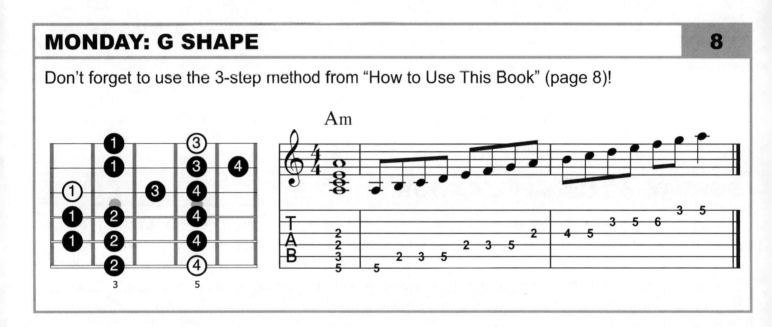

TUESDAY: E SHAPE 9

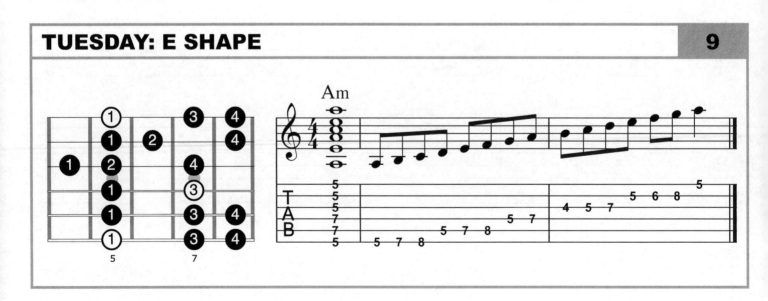

WEDNESDAY: D SHAPE

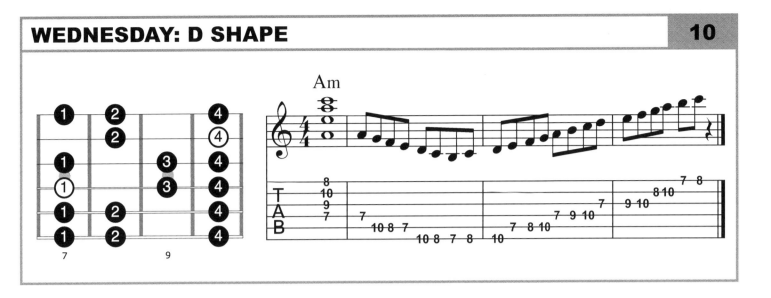

THURSDAY: C SHAPE

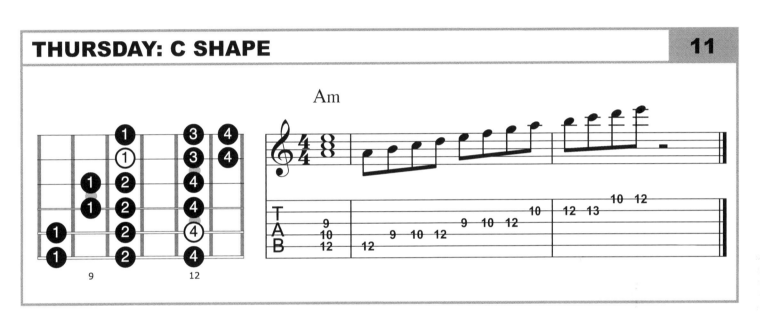

FRIDAY: A SHAPE

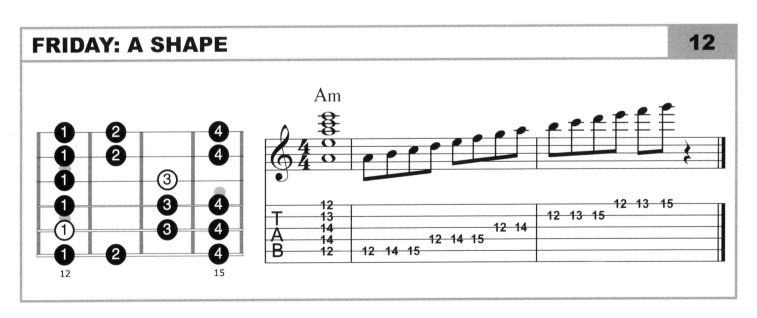

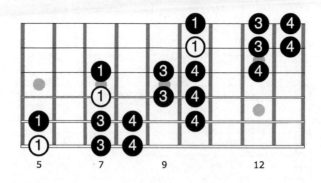

SUNDAY: SCALE APPLICATION   14

Today's melody uses the E Shape and stepwise motion. In addition to the sad, serious minor tonality, this melody features a repeating rhythm figure that is two measures long. Feel free to play it several times in a row, then experiment with your own ideas.

WEEK 3: A MAJOR PENTATONIC

The *major pentatonic scale* is extremely popular. It shares the same notes as the major scale but the 4th and 7th scale degrees are removed, enabling it to be used over many different chords. Let's examine how it's constructed.

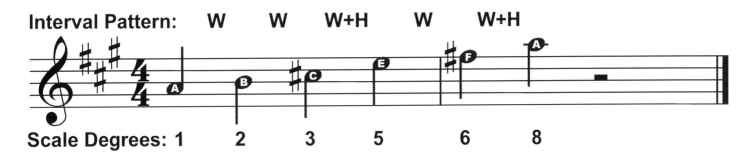

Interval Pattern: W W W+H W W+H

Scale Degrees: 1 2 3 5 6 8

MONDAY: G SHAPE   15

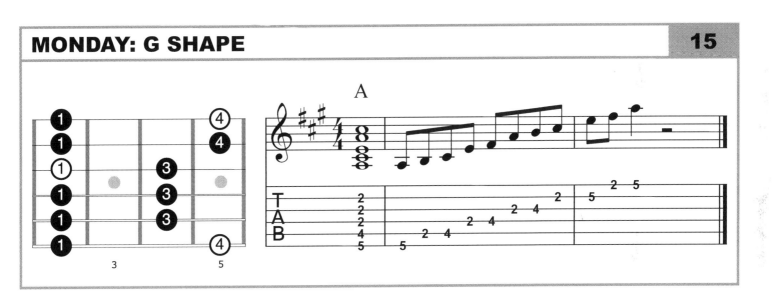

TUESDAY: E SHAPE   16

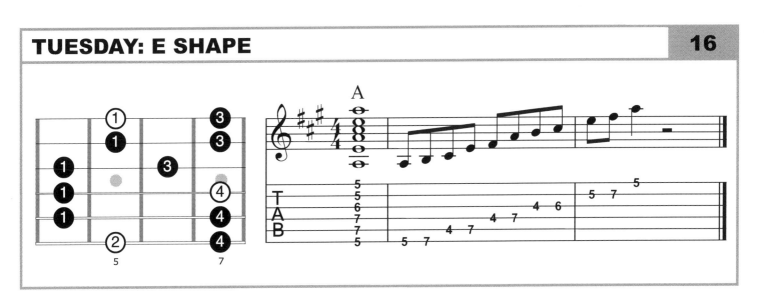

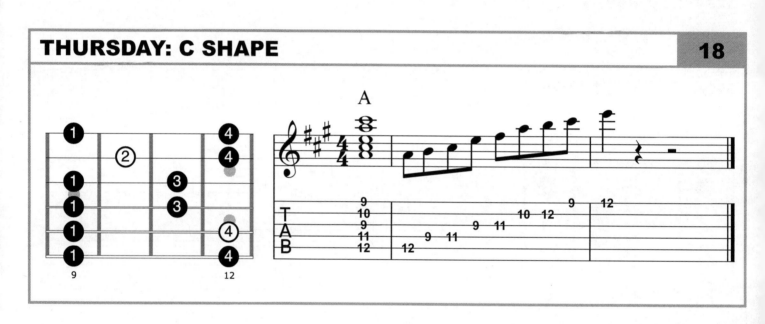

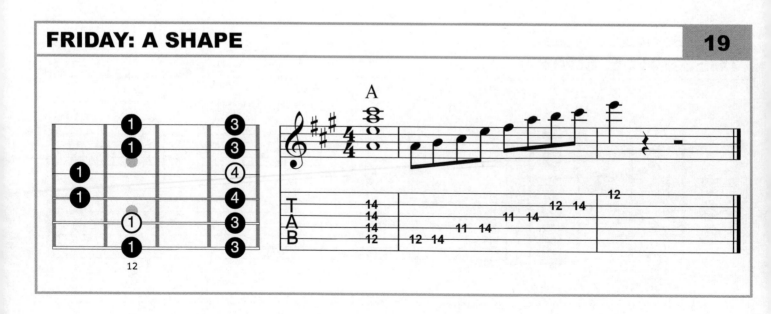

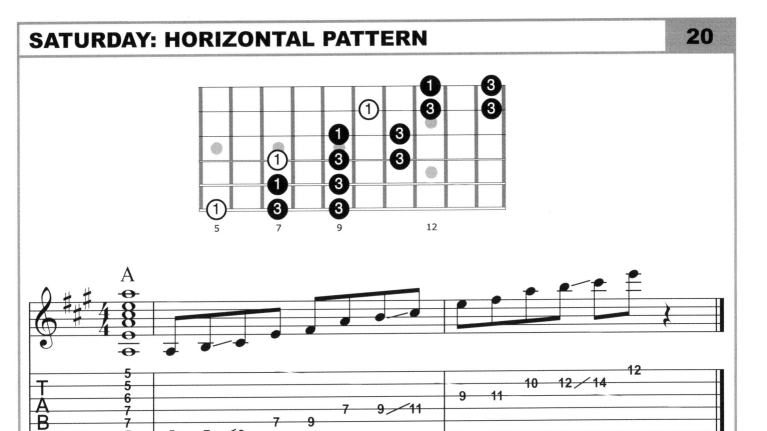

SUNDAY: SCALE APPLICATION 21

Here's an idea you'll find in many guitar solos across multiple styles of music. This pattern is often called a "scale sequence" and uses stepwise motion. Notice how the pattern descends three notes, moves up one note, and then continues this sequence throughout the length of the entire G-Shape scale pattern. When using this in a musical setting, you can use smaller portions of the sequence to move between ideas. Also, you can apply this scale sequence to any of the scale fingerings for extra study.

WEEK 4: A MINOR PENTATONIC

Another extremely popular scale is the *minor pentatonic scale*. It shares the same notes as the minor scale but the 2nd and 6th scale degrees are removed, enabling it to be used over many different chords. Let's examine how it's constructed.

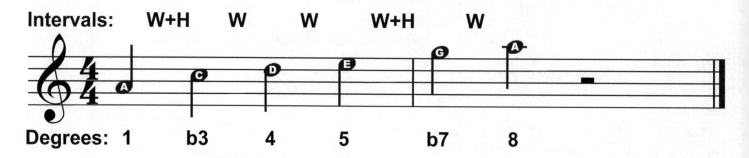

MONDAY: G SHAPE   22

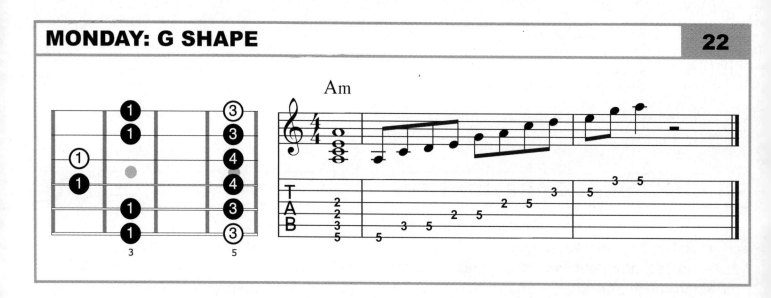

TUESDAY: E SHAPE   23

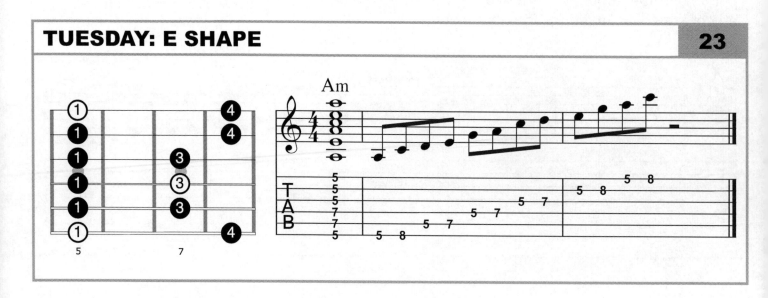

WEDNESDAY: D SHAPE

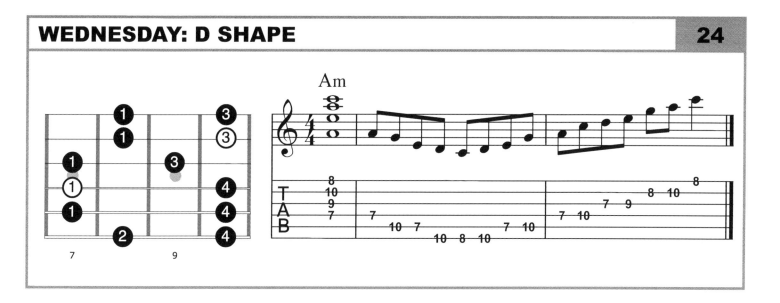

THURSDAY: C SHAPE

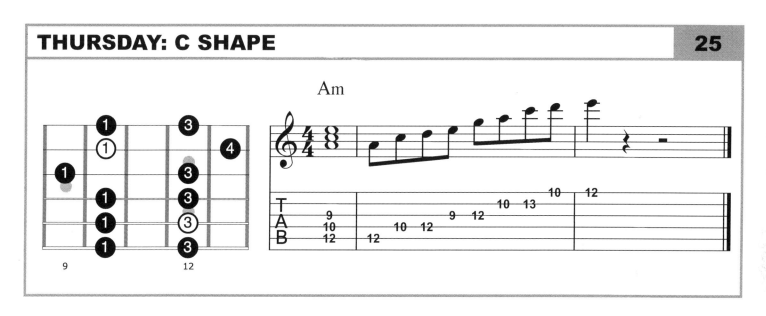

FRIDAY: A SHAPE

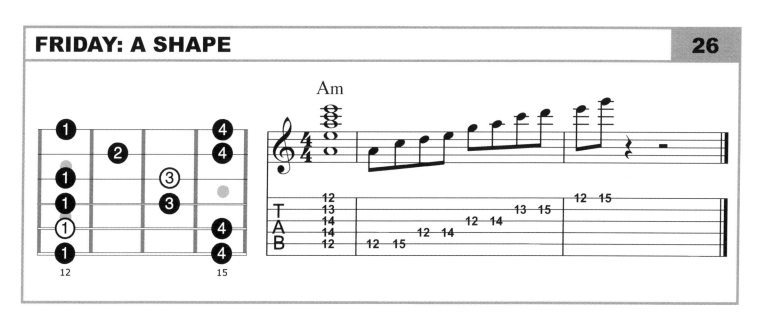

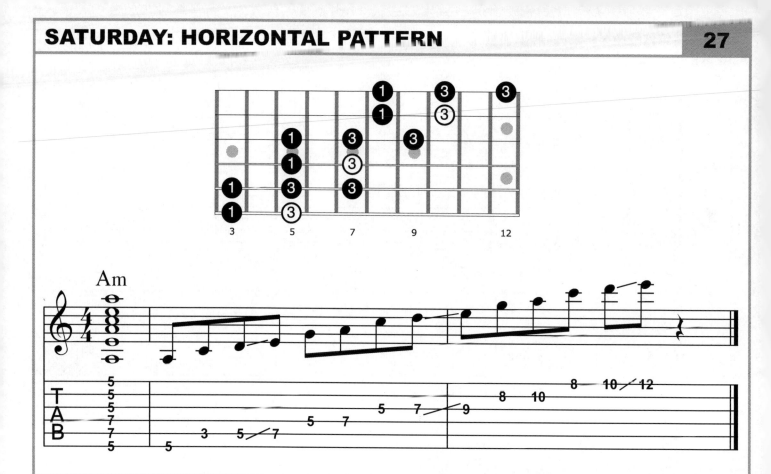

Here's a new stepwise scale sequence that is used in many guitar solos. This one walks up the scale via a 3-note pattern. You can think of it as a starting note that moves down one scale step and then back up to the orginal note. This sequence then moves up one scale step and is repeated several times while ascending the scale. Listening to and playing the example will clarify things. Today, we're using the Horizontal Pattern, but you can apply this pattern to any of the CAGED shapes. You can also start the sequence on any note of the scale and use smaller pieces of the pattern.

WEEK 5: B♭ MAJOR

Congratulations, you've made it through your first key! One of the guitar's challenges is playing the same patterns in different keys, as it can be visually awkward when you're on or off the fretboard dots. Fortunately, the fingerings remain the same. Let's examine how our new scale, B♭ major, is constructed.

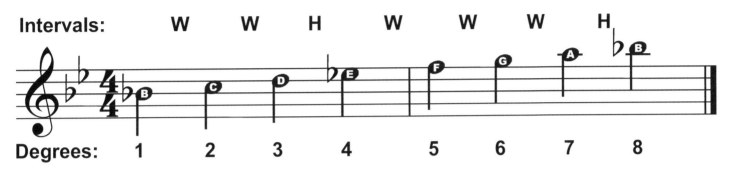

MONDAY: G SHAPE — 29

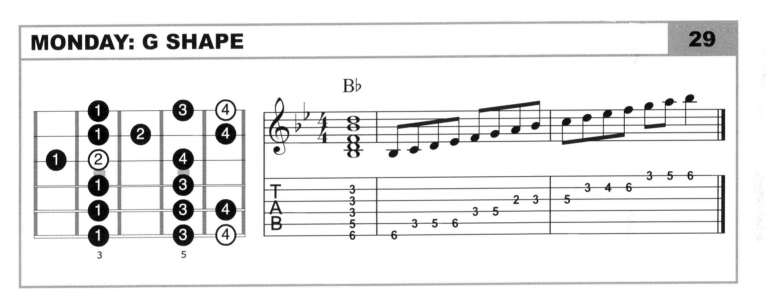

TUESDAY: E SHAPE — 30

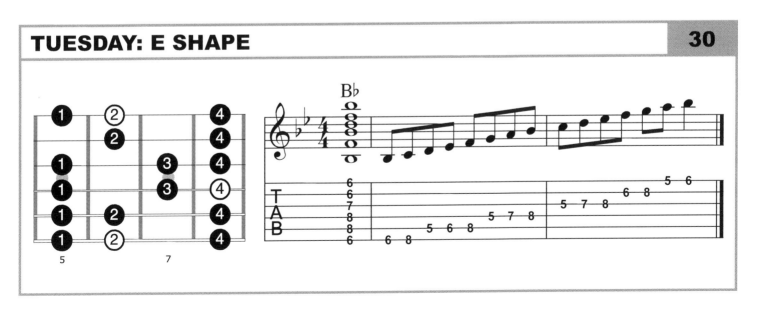

WEDNESDAY: D SHAPE 31

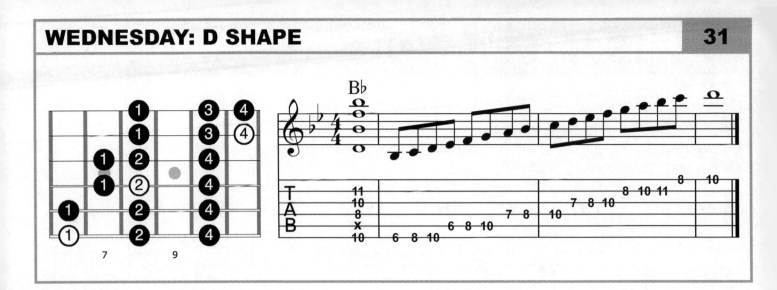

THURSDAY: C SHAPE 32

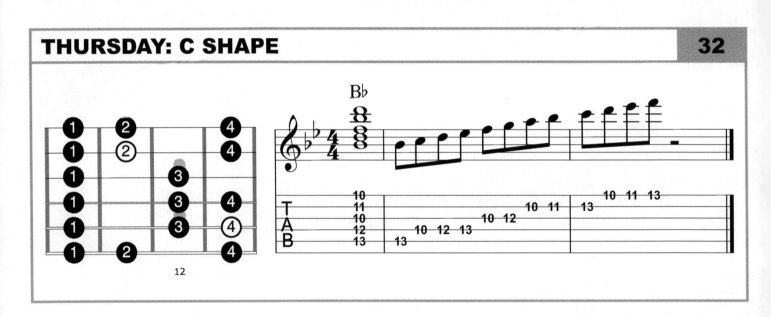

FRIDAY: A SHAPE 33

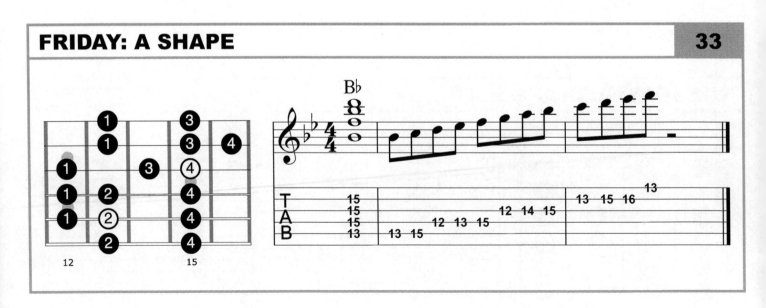

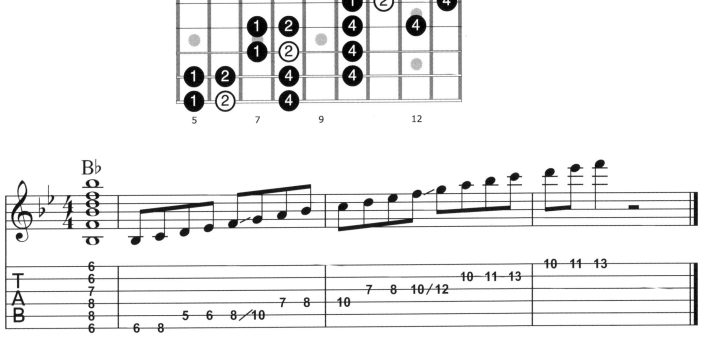

SUNDAY: SCALE APPLICATION

Until this point, we've only used stepwise motion. We'll mix things up a bit here by playing the E-Shape Bb major scale in "3rds". A *3rd interval* involves skipping one note of the scale; for example, the 1st note to the 3rd note, or the 2nd note to the 4th. Many melodies use skips of a 3rd. Feel free to apply 3rds to other scale shapes.

WEEK 6: B♭ MINOR

Interval Pattern:	W	H	W	W	H	W	W

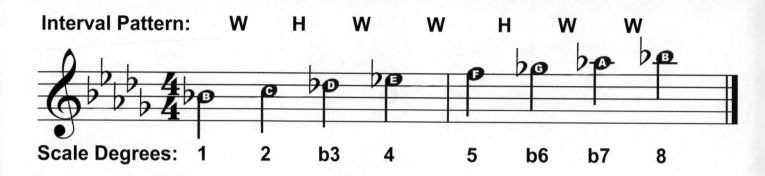

Scale Degrees:	1	2	b3	4	5	b6	b7	8

MONDAY: A SHAPE   36

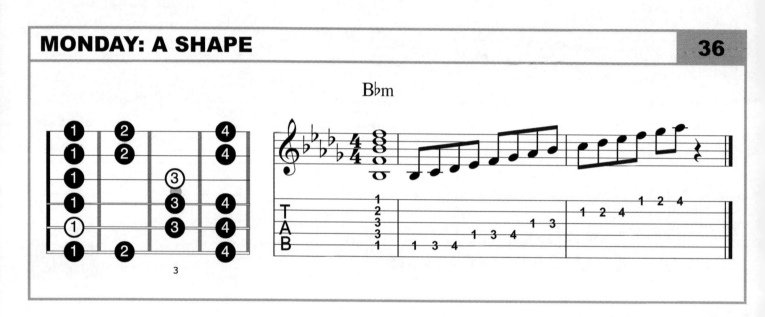

TUESDAY: G SHAPE   37

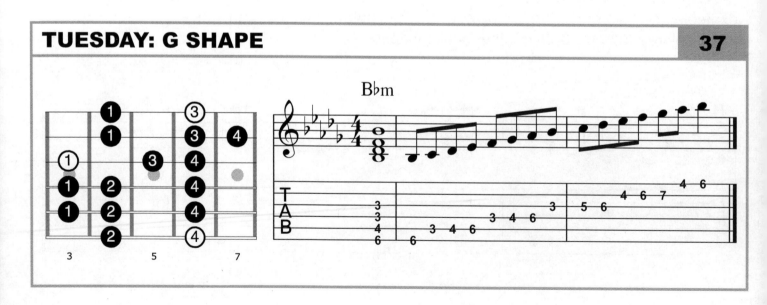

WEDNESDAY: E SHAPE

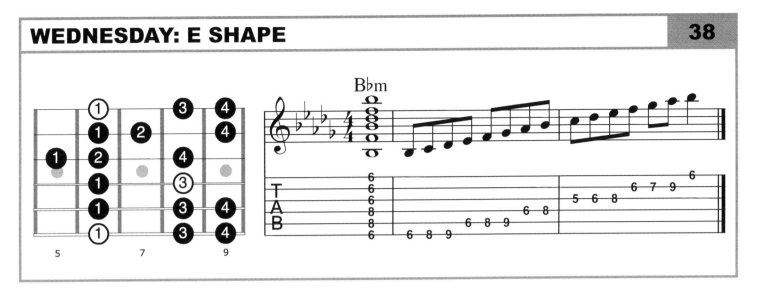

THURSDAY: D SHAPE

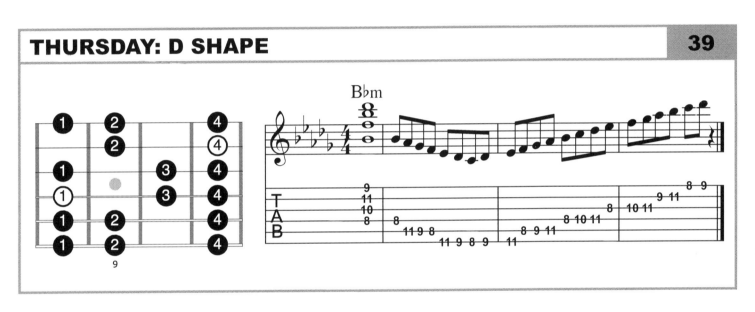

FRIDAY: C SHAPE

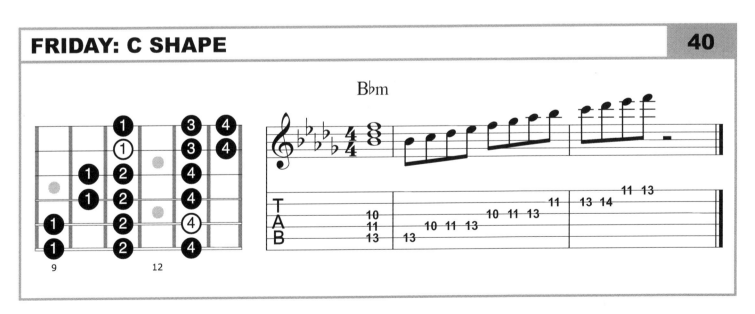

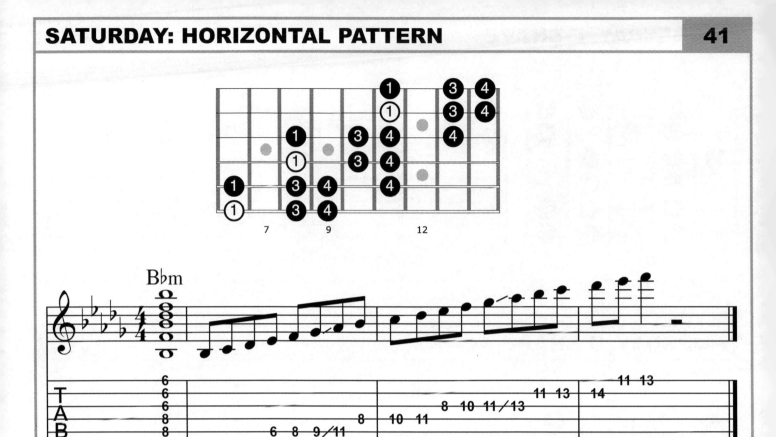

As you might expect, 3rd intervals can also move in descending fashion. Our next exercise does exactly that while using the A-Shape B♭ minor scale. After learning the exercise, try working 3rds into your own melodies.

WEEK 7: B♭ MAJOR PENTATONIC

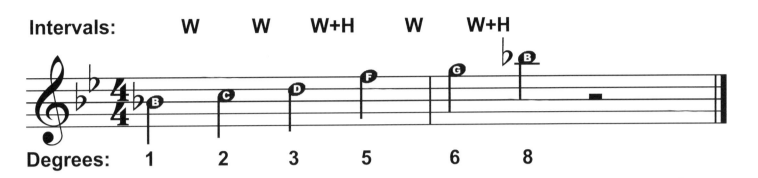

Intervals: W   W   W+H   W   W+H

Degrees: 1   2   3   5   6   8

MONDAY: G SHAPE   43

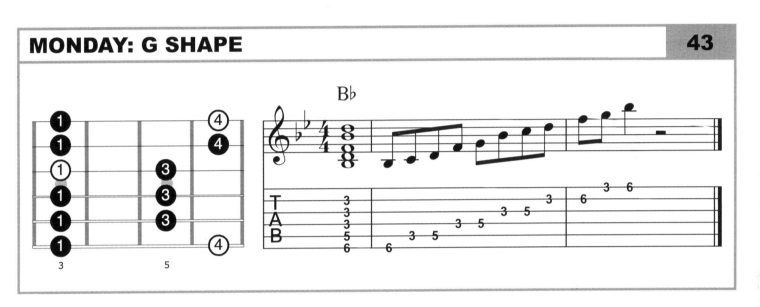

TUESDAY: E SHAPE   44

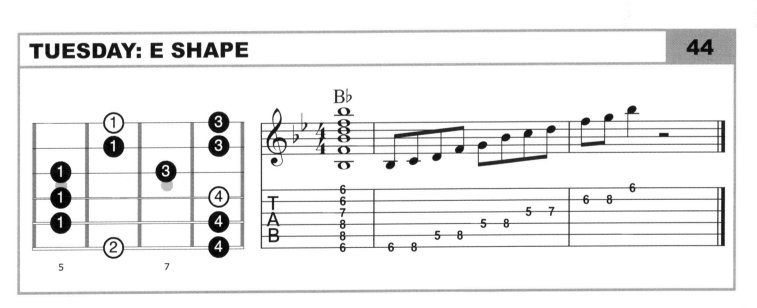

WEDNESDAY: D SHAPE

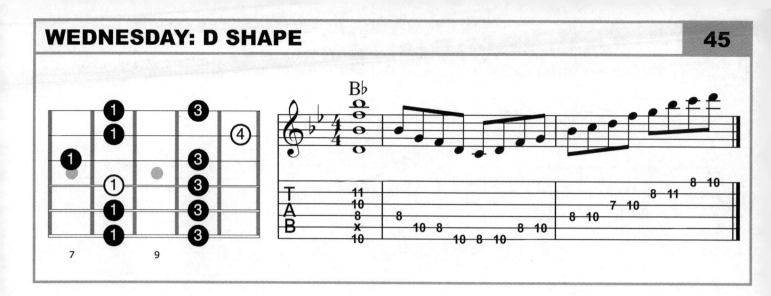

THURSDAY: C SHAPE

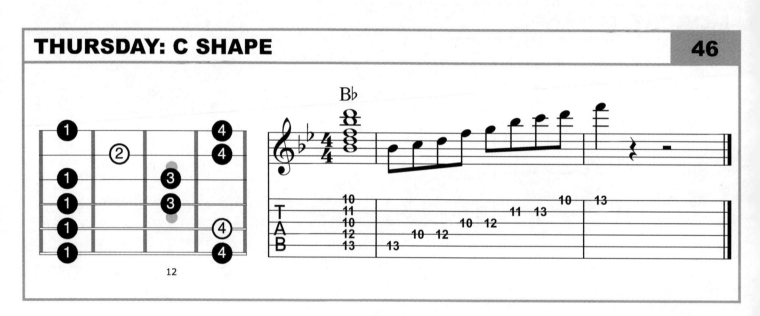

FRIDAY: A SHAPE

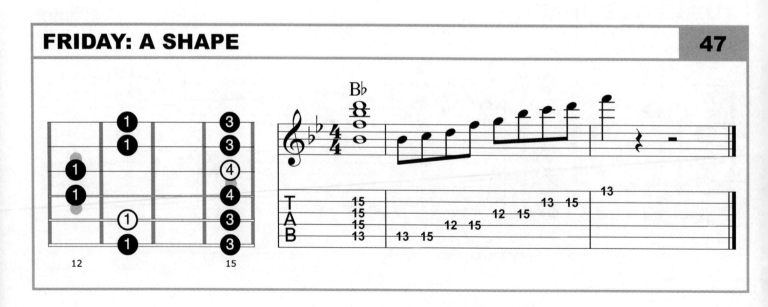

SATURDAY: HORIZONTAL PATTERN

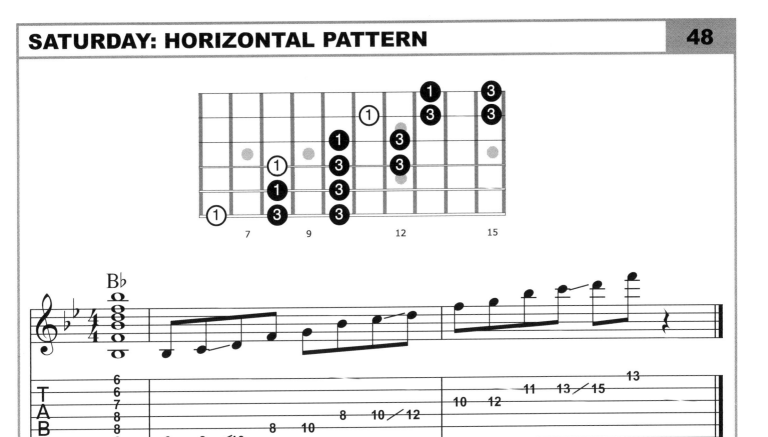

SUNDAY: SCALE APPLICATION

Sometimes creating a melodic theme can be as easy as shifting an idea to a new set of strings within a scale pattern. Notice how this melody starts on the 5th string, ascends four notes, takes a pause, ascends one note to the 3rd string, then resolves back to string 4. This pattern is then moved to string 4 (bar 2) and string 3 (bar 3). In measure 4, try rolling your 3rd finger from string 2 to string 1 on fret 8.

WEEK 8: B♭ MINOR PENTATONIC

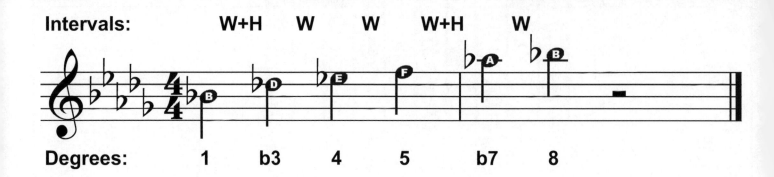

Intervals:	W+H	W	W	W+H	W
Degrees:	1 b3	4	5	b7	8

MONDAY: A SHAPE   50

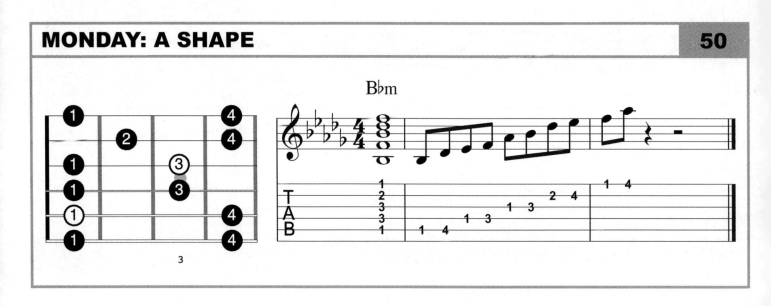

TUESDAY: G SHAPE   51

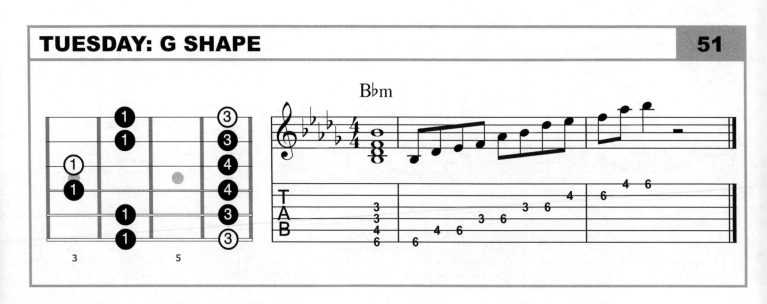

30

WEDNESDAY: E SHAPE

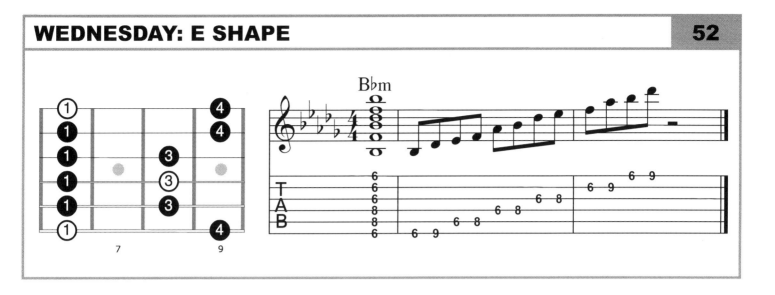

THURSDAY: D SHAPE

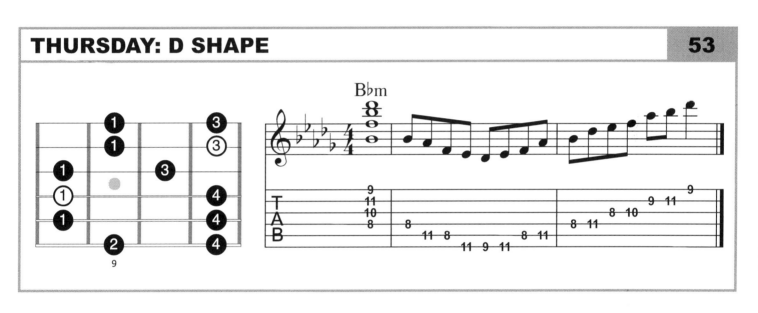

FRIDAY: C SHAPE

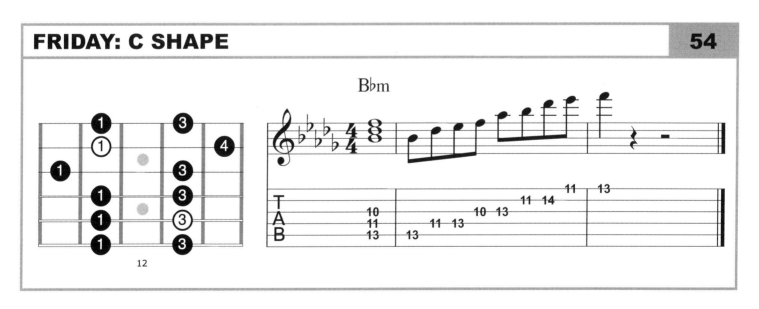

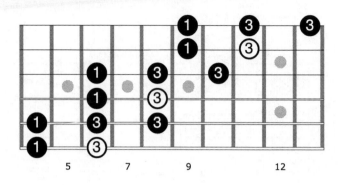

Staying with the idea of moving a phrase to a new set of strings, today's exercise is similar to last Sunday's. However, this phrase descends the scale and uses the G Shape. You can think of this repeating pattern as moving down four notes and then back up two notes. For further study, try this idea with each of the CAGED patterns.

WEEK 9: B MAJOR

Interval Pattern:	W	W	H	W	W	W	H
Scale Degrees: 1	2	3	4	5	6	7	8

MONDAY: A SHAPE 57

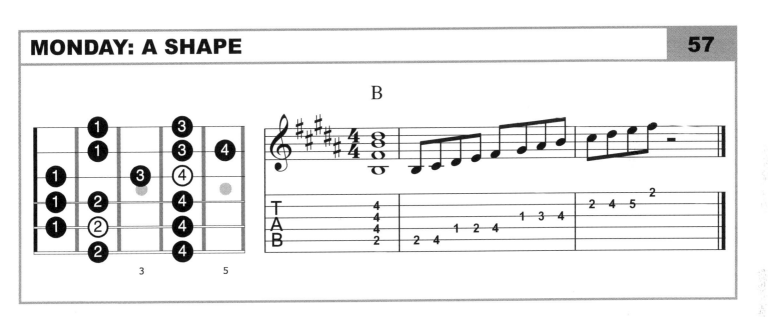

TUESDAY: G SHAPE 58

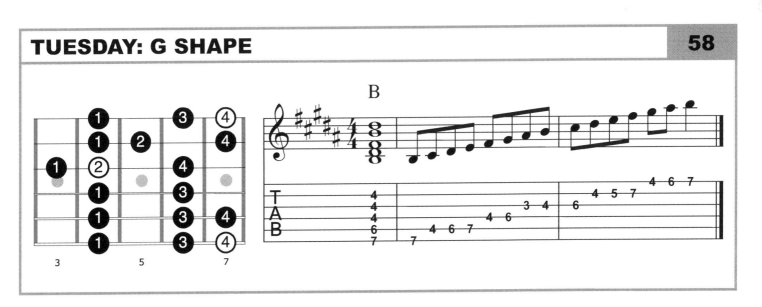

WEDNESDAY: E SHAPE

THURSDAY: D SHAPE

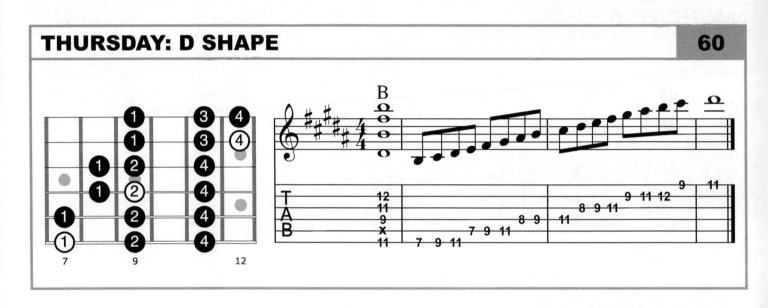

FRIDAY: C SHAPE

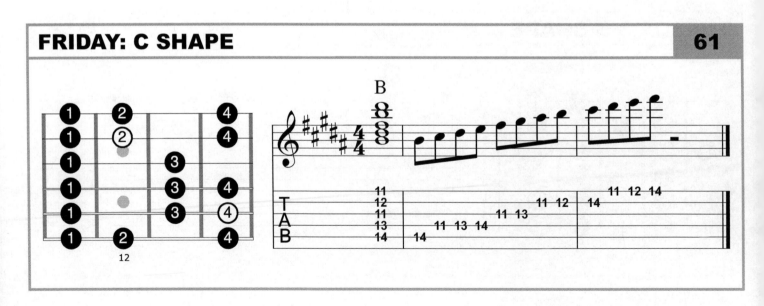

SATURDAY: HORIZONTAL PATTERN

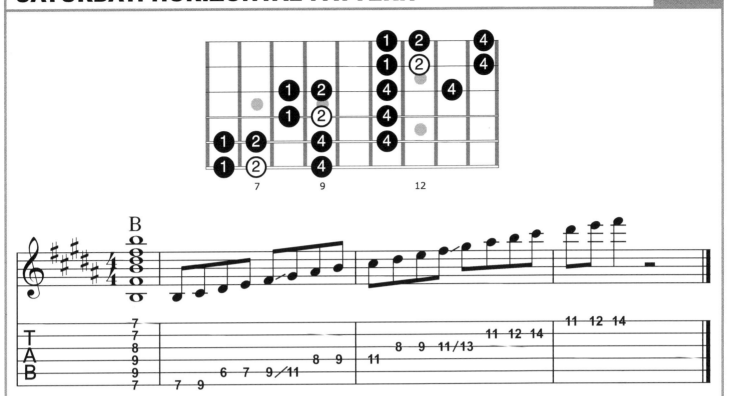

SUNDAY: SCALE APPLICATION

Major scales can be played in stepwise groups of 3, as well. When writing or improvising a melody, patterns such as this are great for connecting phrases or moving to a different octave of the scale.

WEEK 10: B MINOR

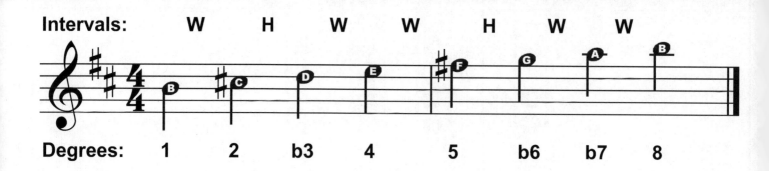

Intervals:	W	H	W	W	H	W	W
Degrees: 1	2	b3	4	5	b6	b7	8

MONDAY: A SHAPE

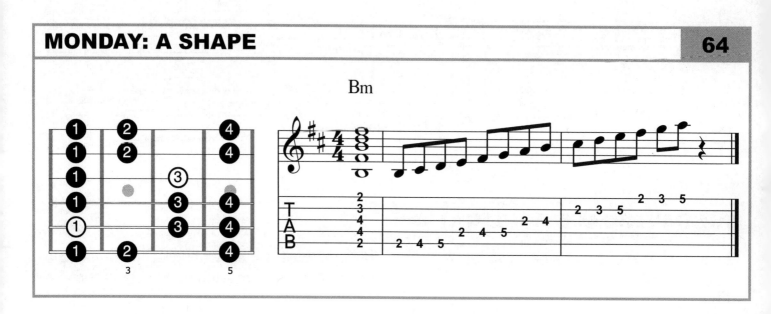

TUESDAY: G SHAPE

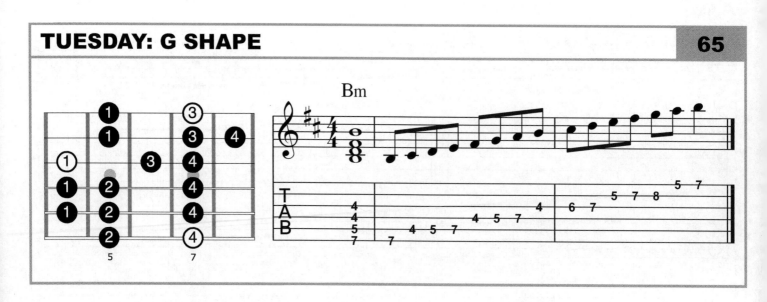

WEDNESDAY: E SHAPE

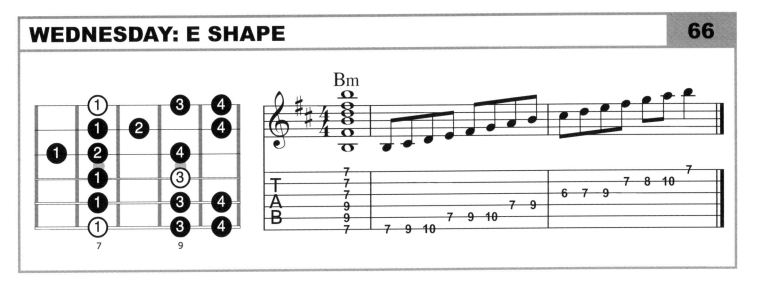

THURSDAY: D SHAPE

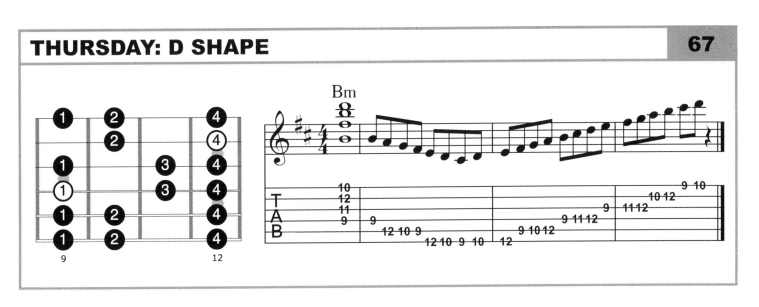

FRIDAY: C SHAPE

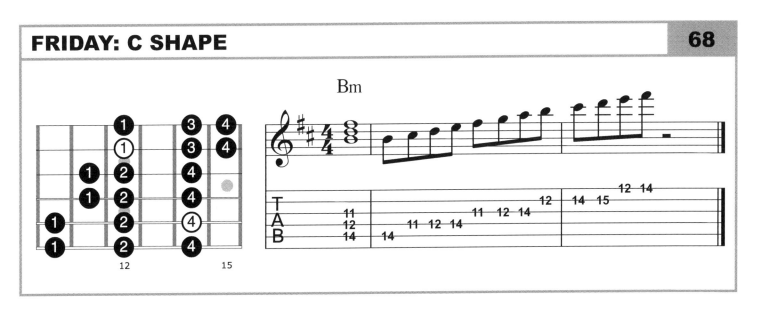

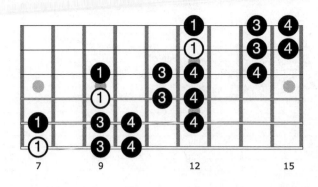

Ascending stepwise in 3s yields the same musical results and benefits as descending. Today's application shares a common fingering with last Sunday's example. However, its fretboard location and starting note have changed, which determines the interval pattern and sound of the scale.

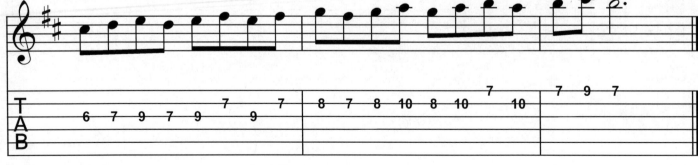

38

WEEK 11: B MAJOR PENTATONIC

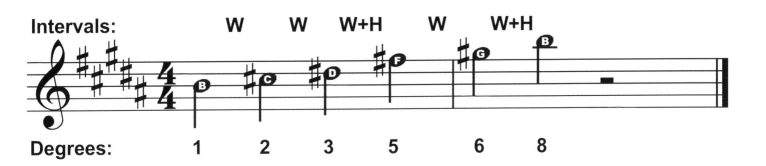

MONDAY: A SHAPE

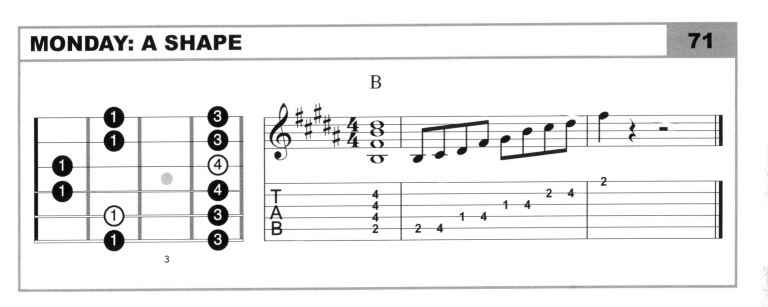

TUESDAY: G SHAPE

WEDNESDAY: E SHAPE

THURSDAY: D SHAPE

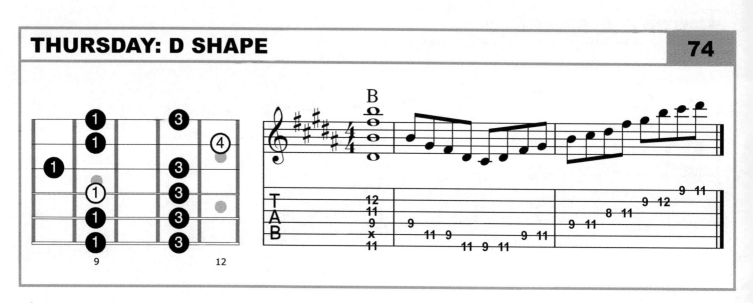

FRIDAY: C SHAPE

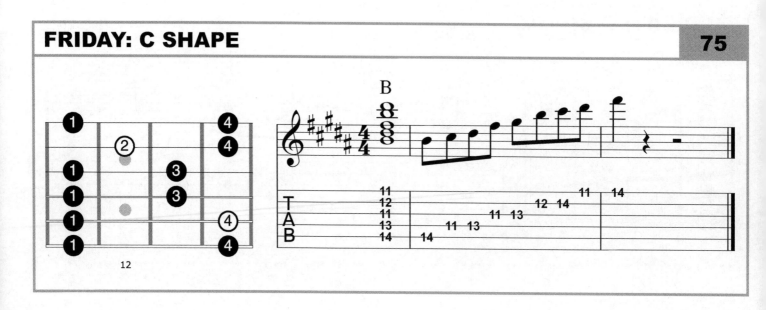

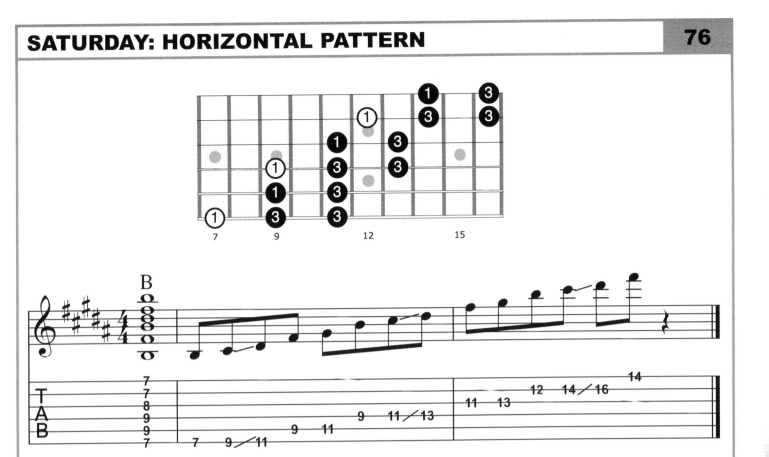

Skipping notes to break up stepwise motion works in the pentatonic scale, as well. Notice how moving the basic idea to new strings and repeating a rhythm helps the melody establish a theme. When crossing strings with the same finger in measures 2–4, try playing the first note with the pad of your 3rd finger and rolling up to the tip for the string below it.

WEEK 12: B MINOR PENTATONIC

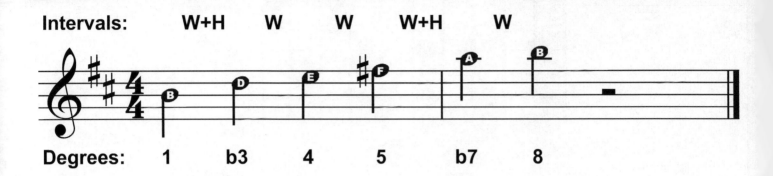

Intervals: W+H W W W+H W

Degrees: 1 b3 4 5 b7 8

MONDAY: A SHAPE   78

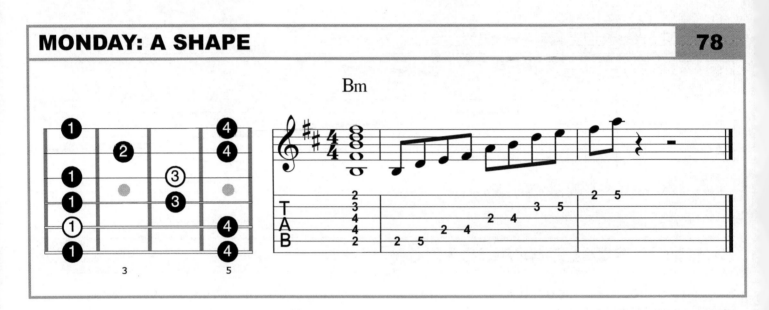

TUESDAY: G SHAPE   79

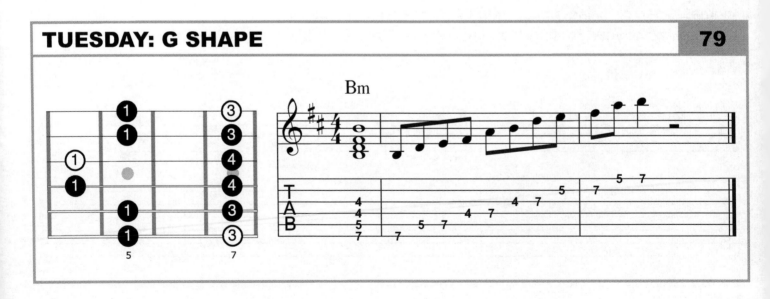

WEDNESDAY: E SHAPE

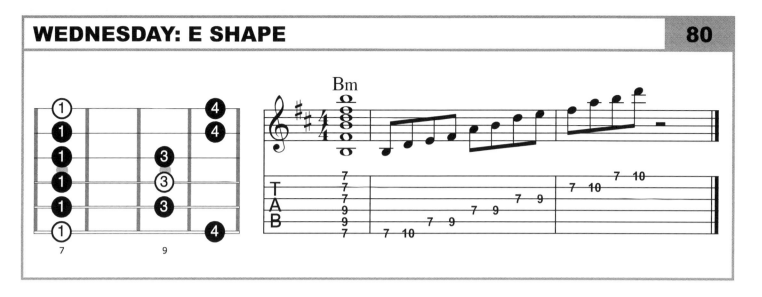

THURSDAY: D SHAPE

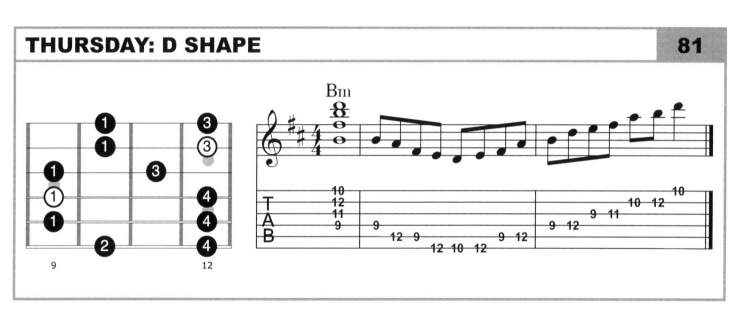

FRIDAY: C SHAPE

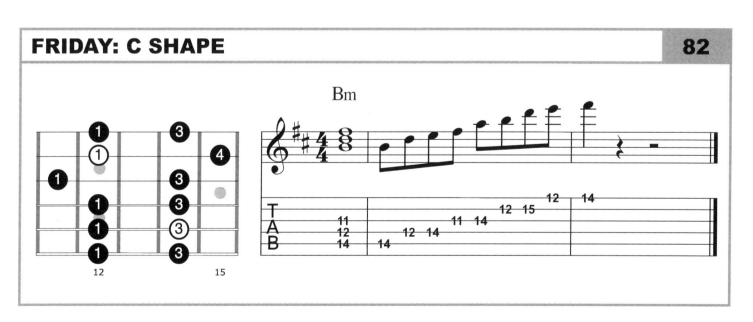

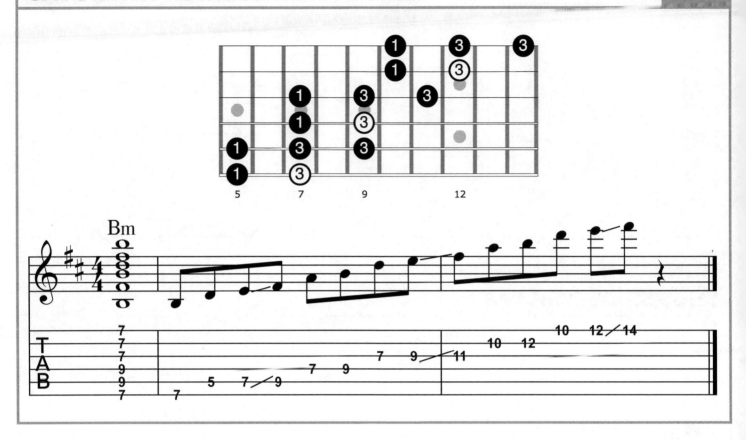

SUNDAY: SCALE APPLICATION   84

The minor pentatonic scale and the blues are historically a perfect fit. This is a popular blues figure that offers an opportunity to practice rolling your 3rd finger. Voice the 4th string with the tip of your 3rd finger and roll it down, collapsing your knuckle to play the 3rd string. Listen to the audio to get the blues shuffle feel.

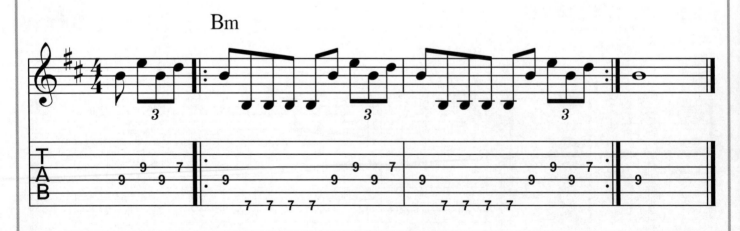

WEEK 13: C MAJOR

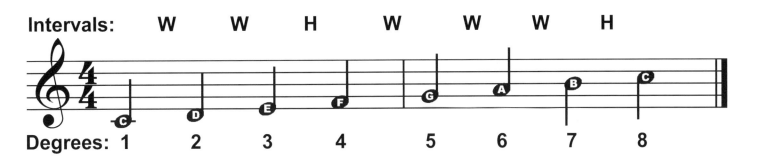

Intervals: W W H W W W H

Degrees: 1 2 3 4 5 6 7 8

MONDAY: A SHAPE 85

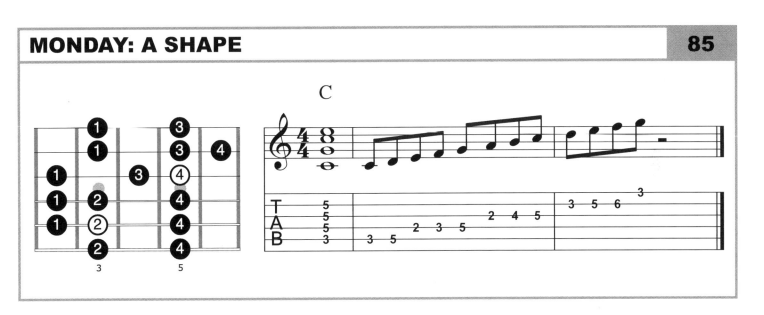

TUESDAY: G SHAPE 86

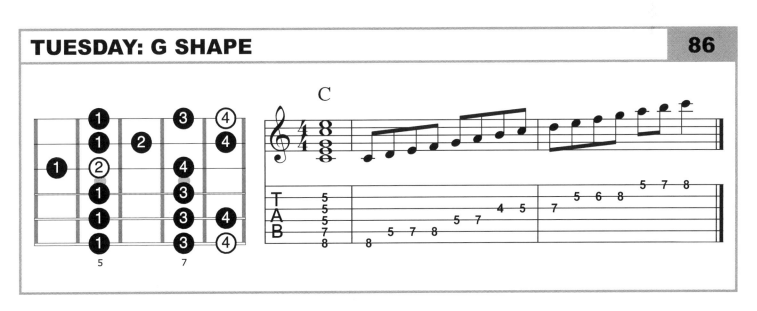

WEDNESDAY: E SHAPE

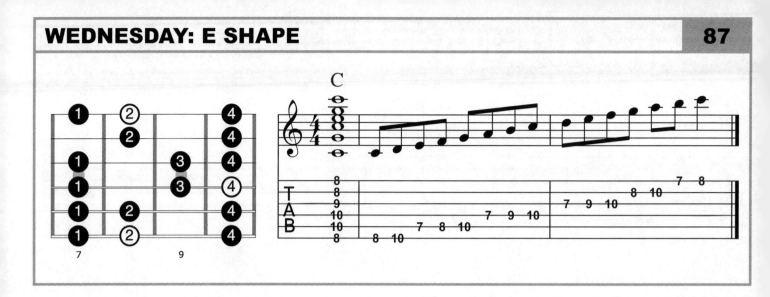

THURSDAY: D SHAPE

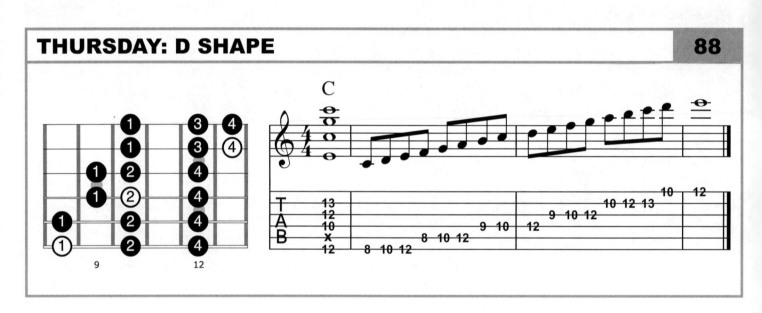

FRIDAY: C SHAPE

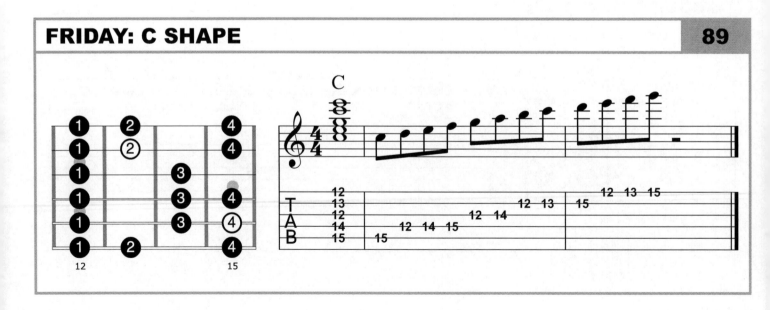

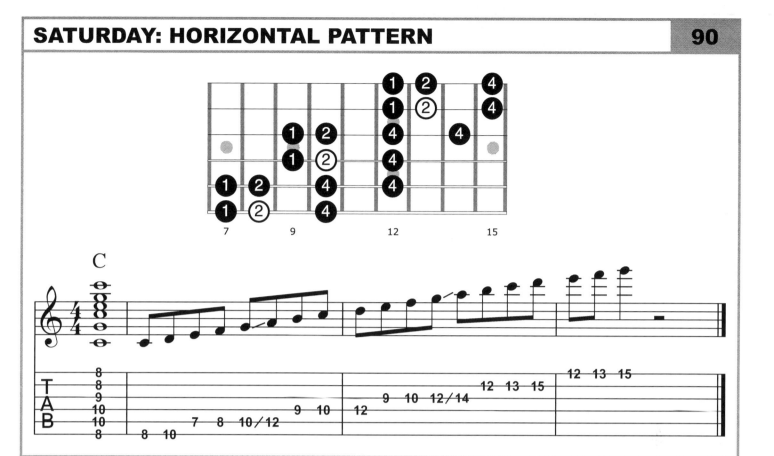

Another common stepwise scale sequence is to use groups of 4. This pattern uses the D-Shape C major scale and is often used for connecting melodic ideas. Practicing it will also help to develop finger dexterity and sync your picking and fretting hands.

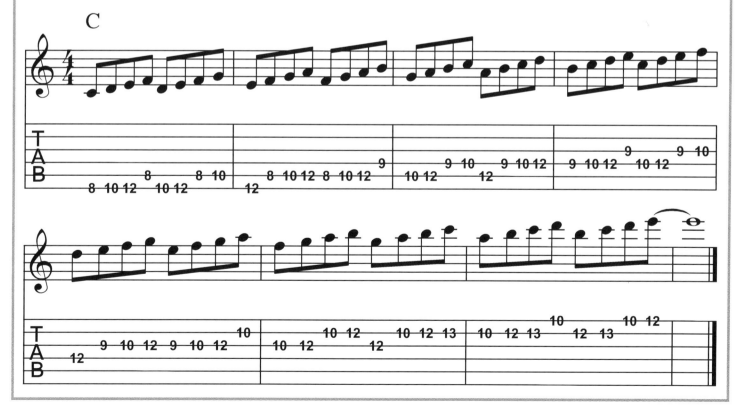

WEEK 14: C MINOR

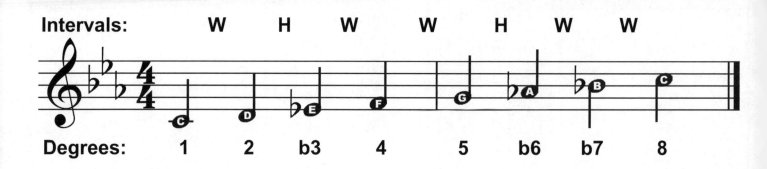

Intervals:	W	H	W	W	H	W	W
Degrees:	1	2	b3	4	5	b6	b7	8

MONDAY: A SHAPE

92

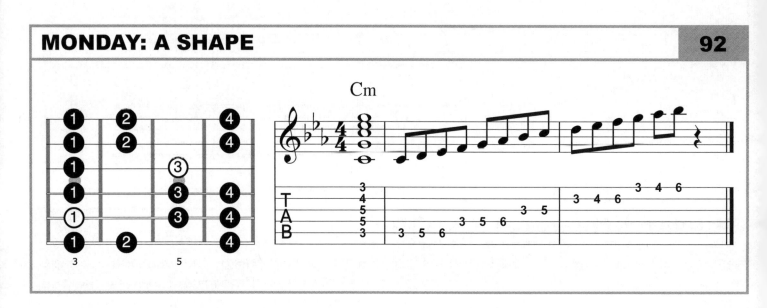

TUESDAY: G SHAPE

93

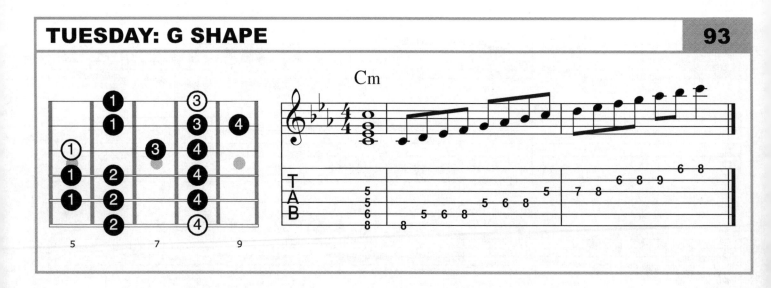

48

WEDNESDAY: E SHAPE

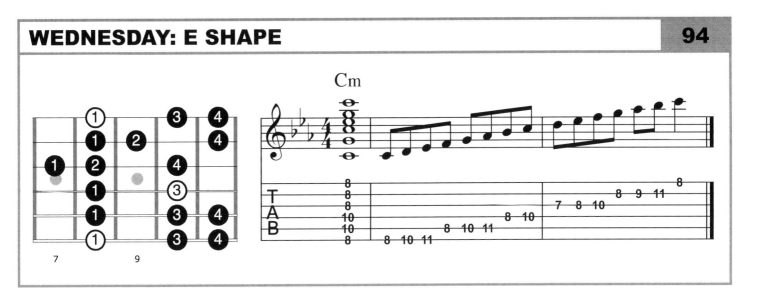

THURSDAY: D SHAPE

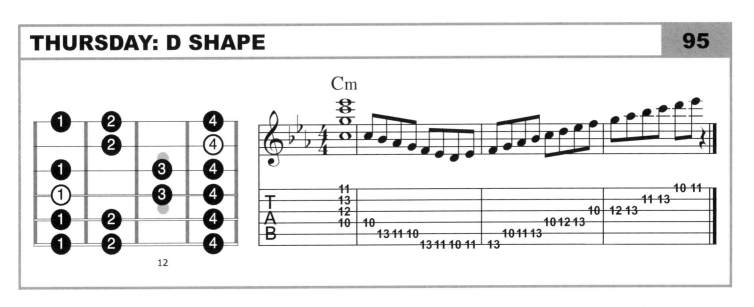

FRIDAY: C SHAPE

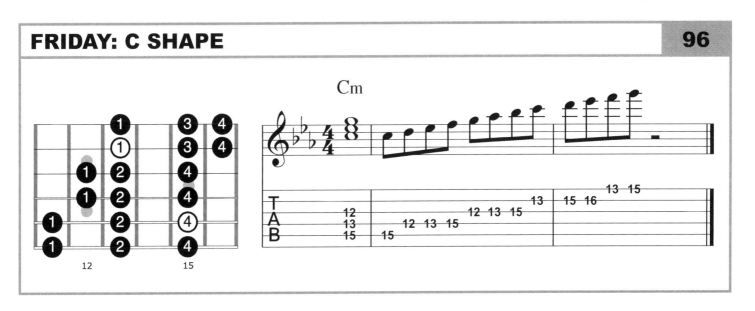

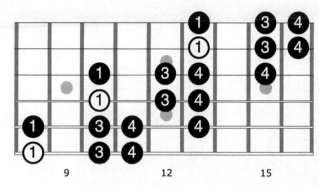

Today's exercise uses the A Shape to explore descending a scale in groups of 4. These patterns are great for combining alternate picking and scale practice. Try to keep your foot and pick going in the same direction: down on the numbers (1, 2, 3, 4), and up on the "ands."

WEEK 15: C MAJOR PENTATONIC

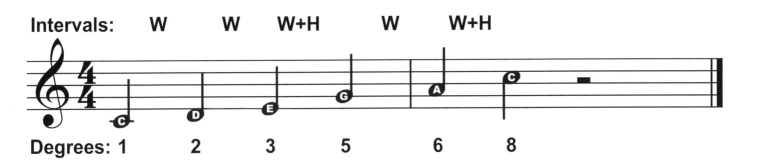

Intervals:		W		W		W+H		W		W+H	

Degrees: 1   2   3   5   6   8

MONDAY: A SHAPE

TUESDAY: G SHAPE

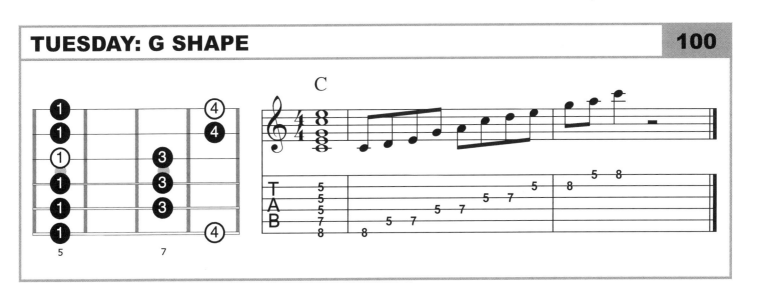

WEDNESDAY: E SHAPE

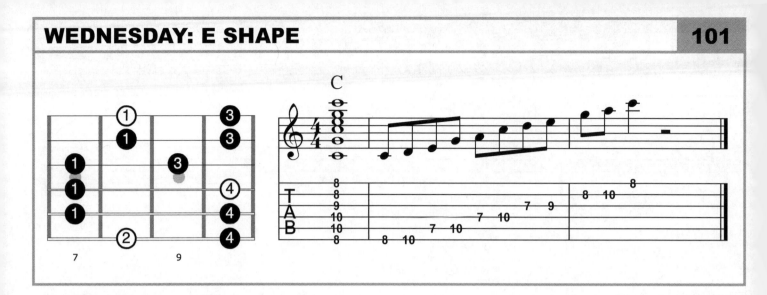

THURSDAY: D SHAPE

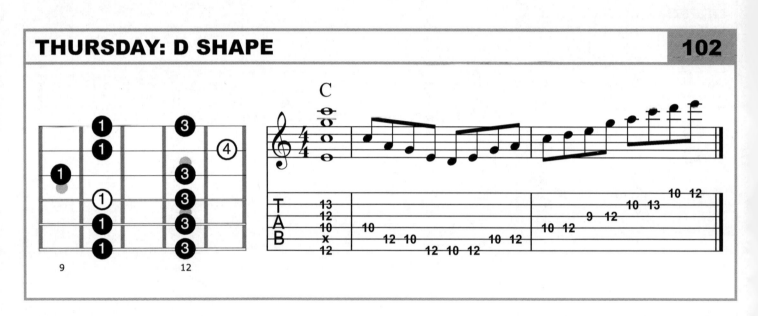

FRIDAY: C SHAPE

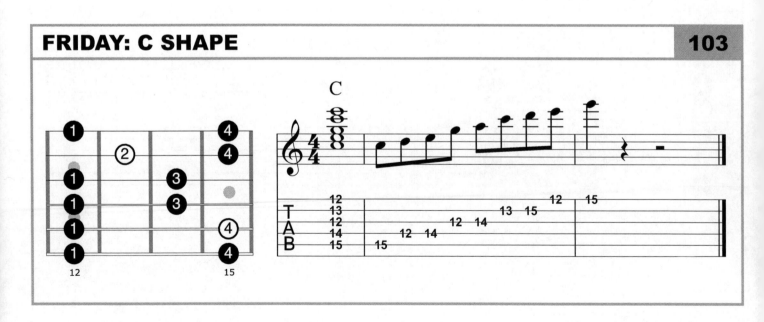

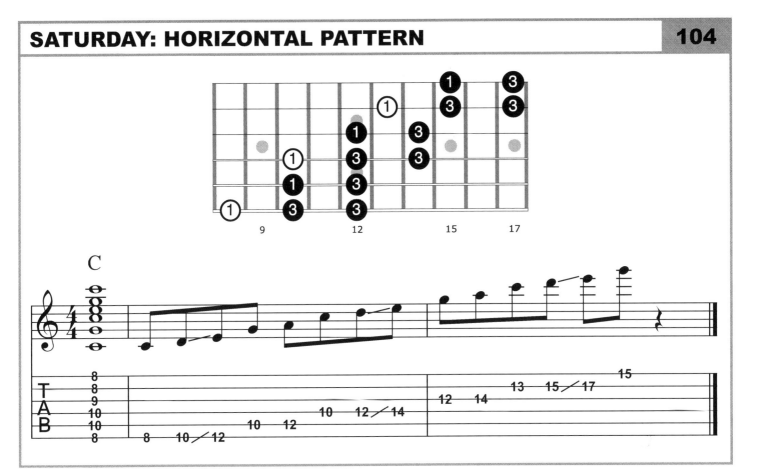

A great attribute of the horizontal pentatonic pattern is the three symmetrical groups of five notes. The following melodic phrase demonstrates how you can apply a single idea to different octaves of the scale to create a theme. Simply changing the last two notes brings the phrase to a conclusion.

WEEK 16: C MINOR PENTATONIC

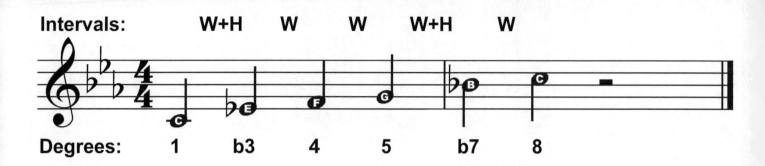

Intervals:	W+H	W	W	W+H	W
Degrees:	1	b3	4	5	b7	8

MONDAY: A SHAPE

106

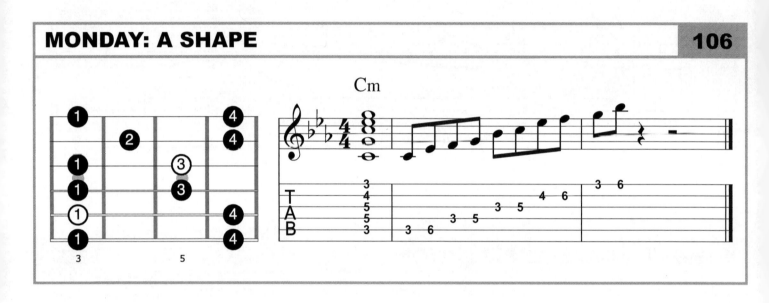

TUESDAY: G SHAPE

107

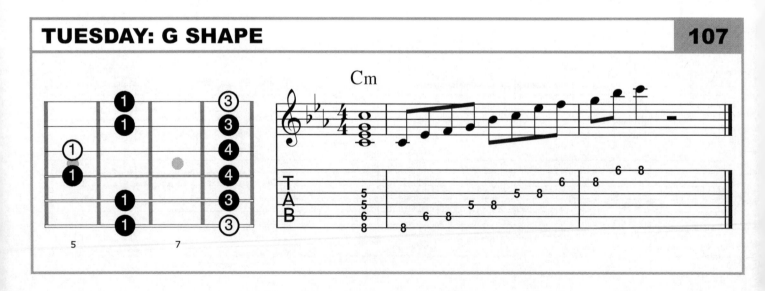

WEDNESDAY: E SHAPE

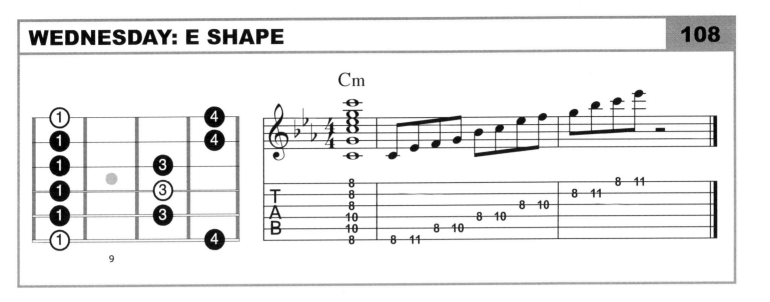

THURSDAY: D SHAPE

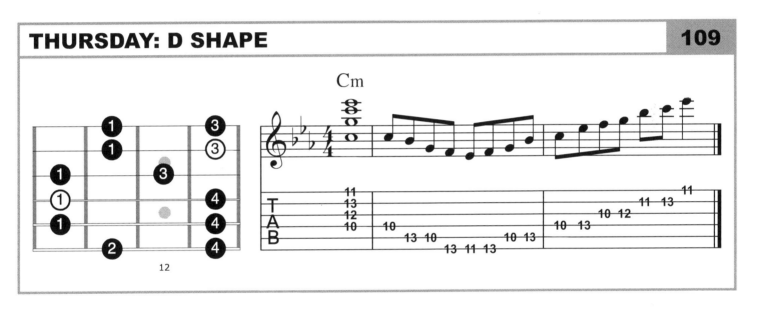

FRIDAY: C SHAPE

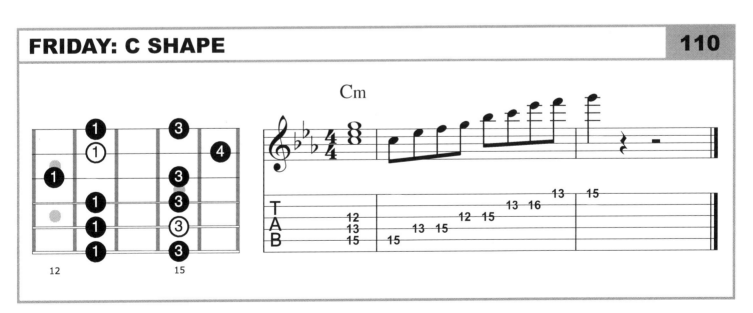

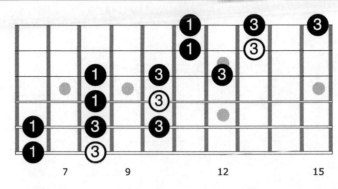

The minor horizontal pentatonic pattern also has three symmetrical groups of five notes. Our next phrase combines the down 3/up 1 scale sequence with triplets and spans three octaves.

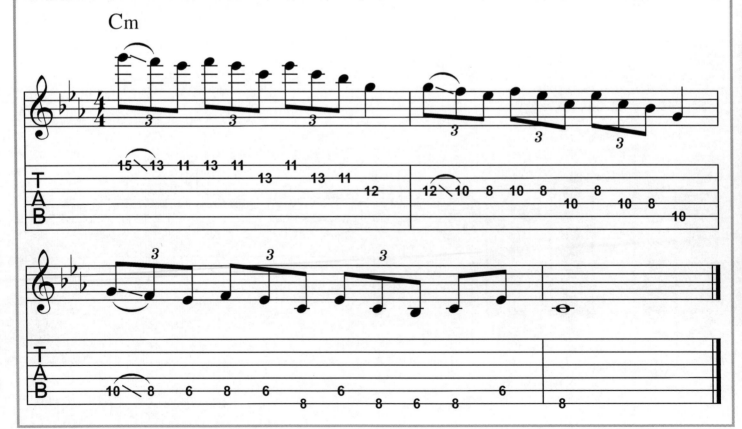

WEEK 17: C♯ MAJOR

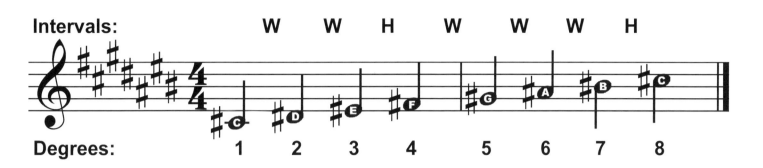

Intervals:		W	W	H	W	W	W	H
Degrees:		1	2	3	4	5	6	7	8

MONDAY: C SHAPE 113

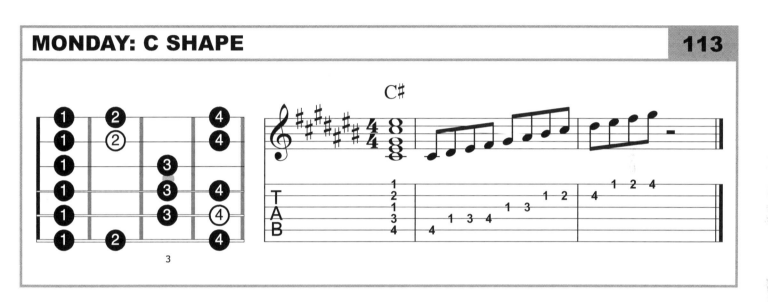

TUESDAY: A SHAPE 114

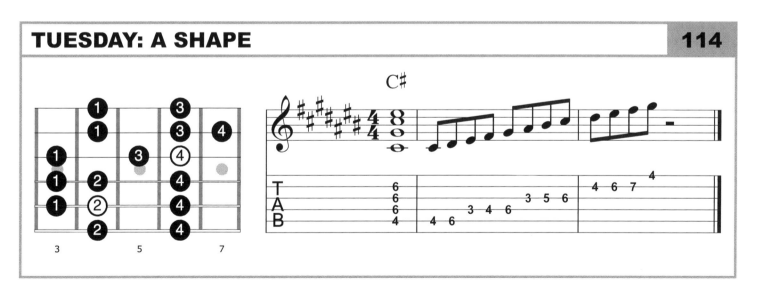

WEDNESDAY: G SHAPE

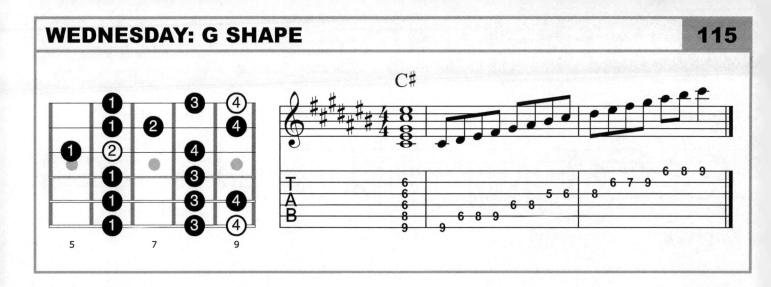

THURSDAY: E SHAPE

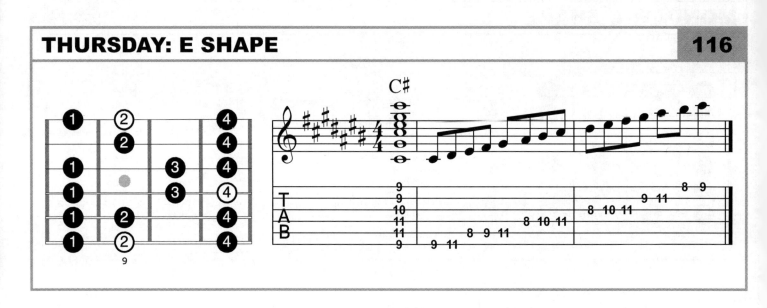

FRIDAY: D SHAPE

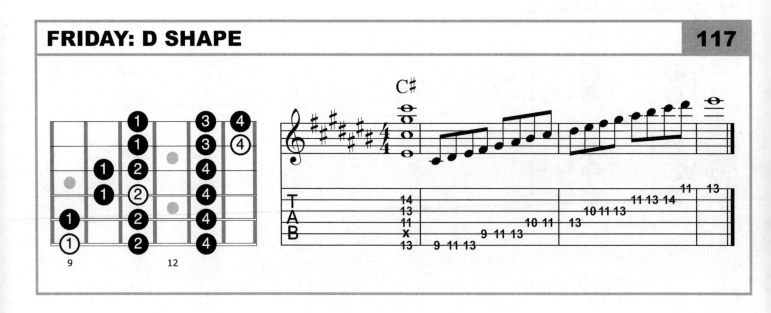

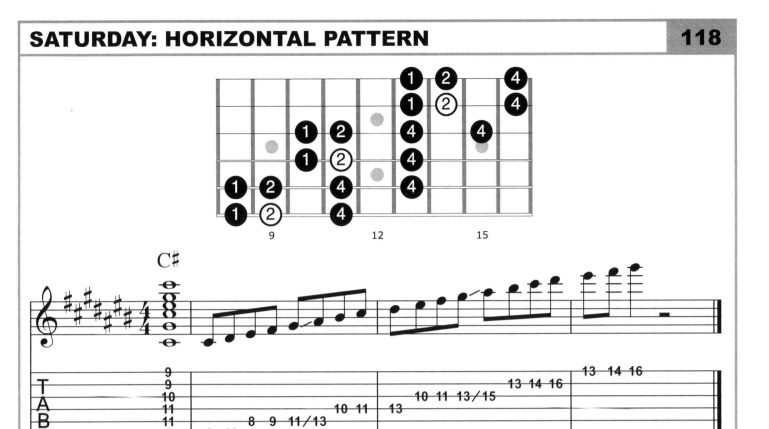

In today's melody, we'll explore tension and release. A *triad* is a chord made up of the root, 3rd, and 5th of a scale. In general, ending on a note used in the chord creates release. When you land on the 2nd, 4th, 6th, or 7th tones of the scale (tension), they usually want to move up or down to a chord tone (release). Notice how the 7th measure creates tension by ending on the 2nd (D#).

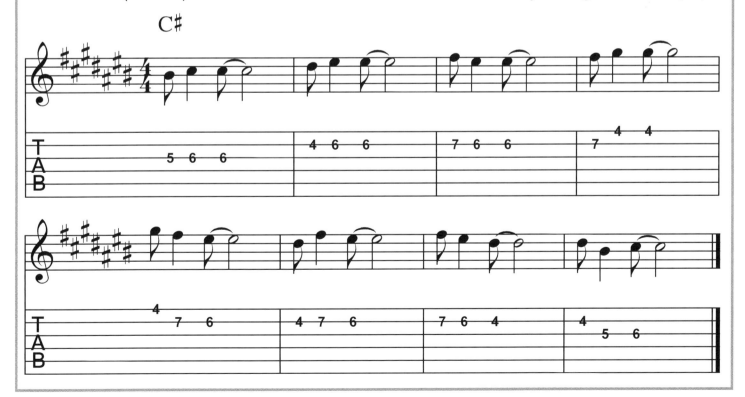

WEEK 18: C♯ MINOR

Intervals:	W	H	W	W	H	W	W
Degrees:	1	2	b3	4	5	b6	b7	8

MONDAY: A SHAPE

120

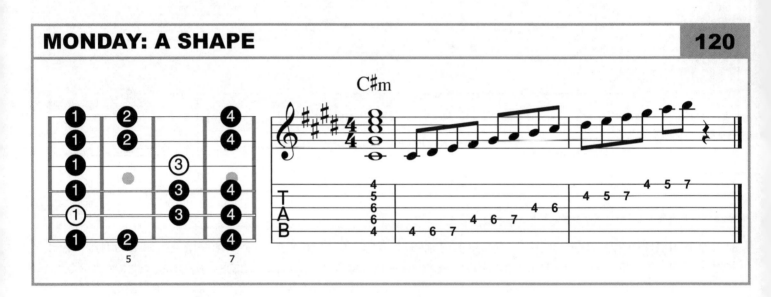

TUESDAY: G SHAPE

121

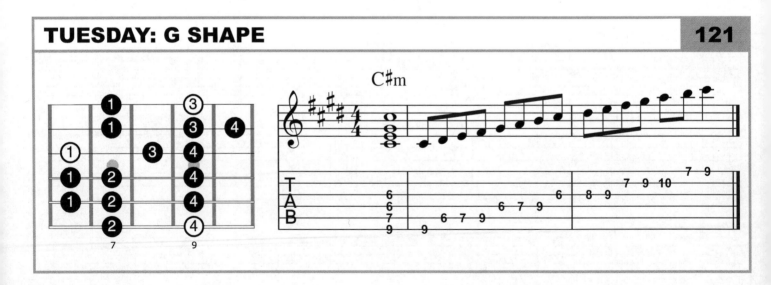

WEDNESDAY: E SHAPE

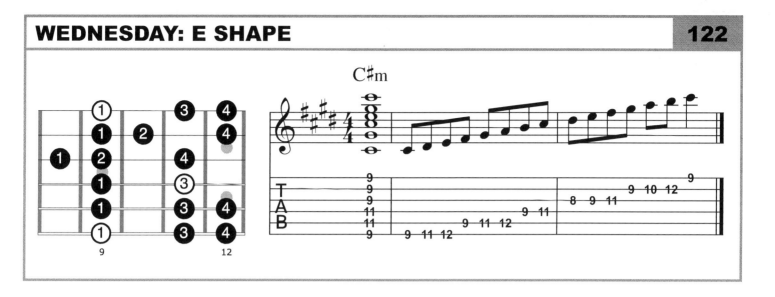

THURSDAY: D SHAPE

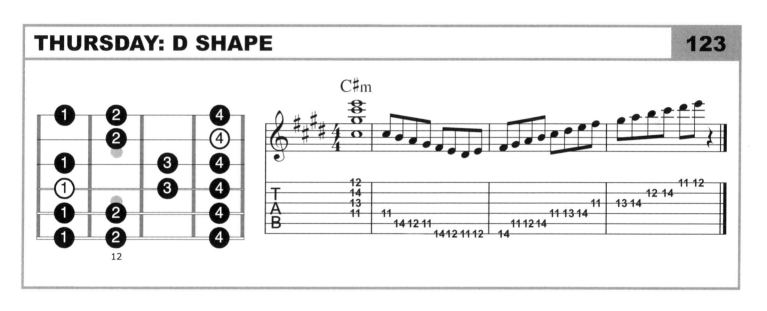

FRIDAY: C SHAPE

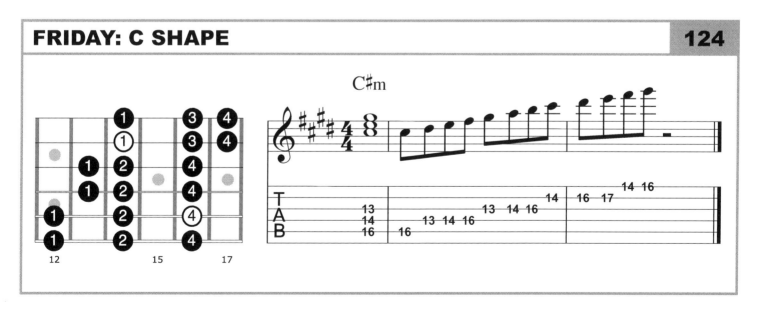

SATURDAY: HORIZONTAL PATTERN

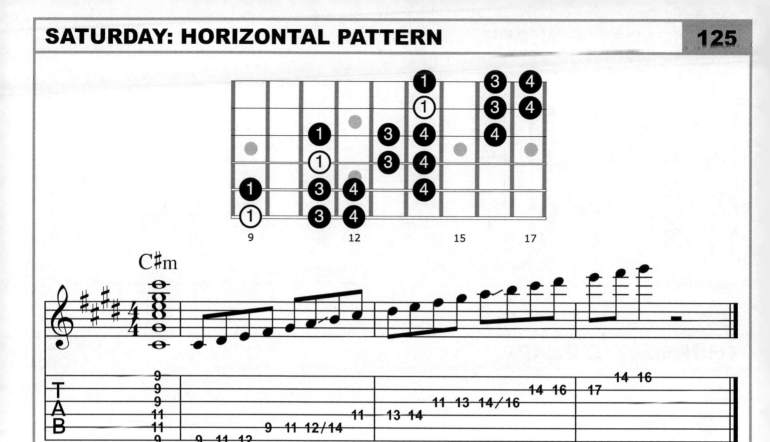

SUNDAY: SCALE APPLICATION

A *riff* is generally a lower-voiced, repeated phrase that is typically used as an introduction or refrain in a song. Here's an example riff that uses the A Shape. Feel free to increase the tempo and add some overdrive as you become comfortable with it.

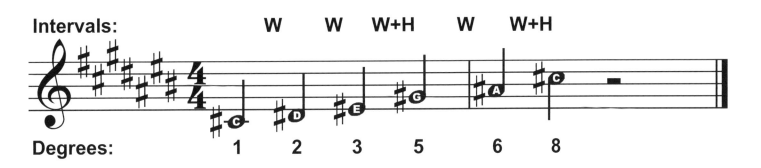

MONDAY: C SHAPE — 127

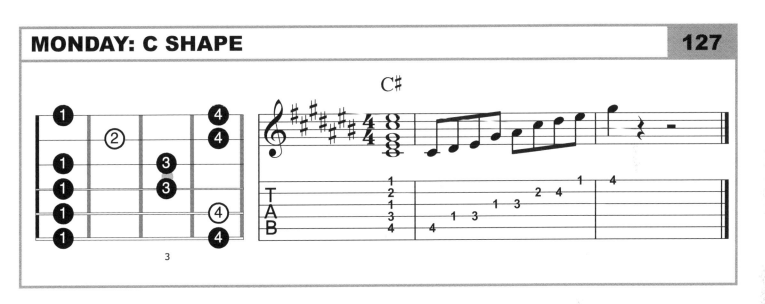

TUESDAY: A SHAPE — 128

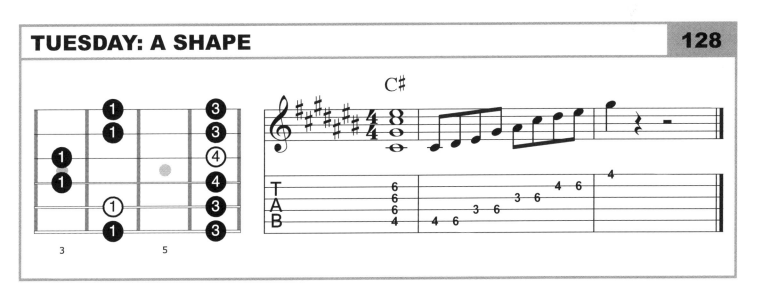

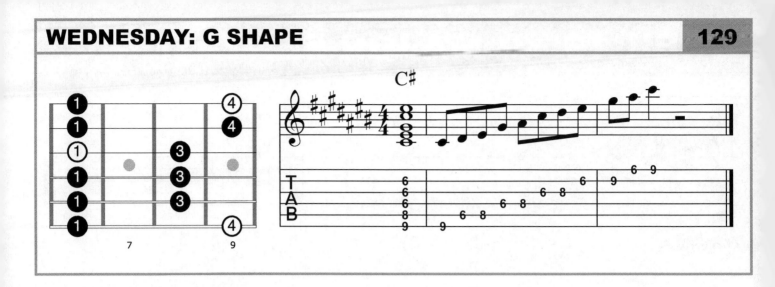

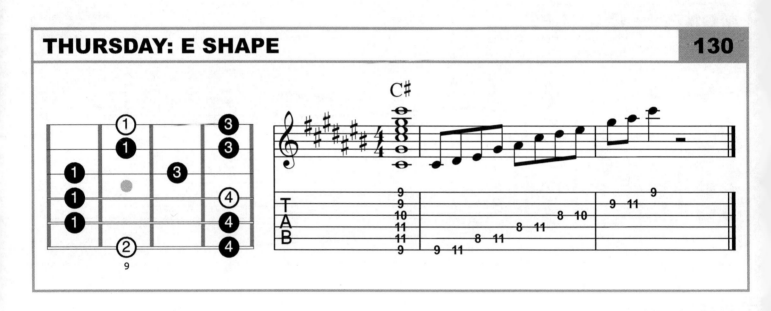

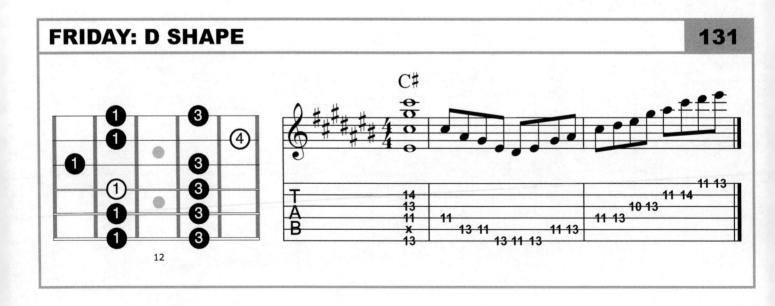

SATURDAY: HORIZONTAL PATTERN

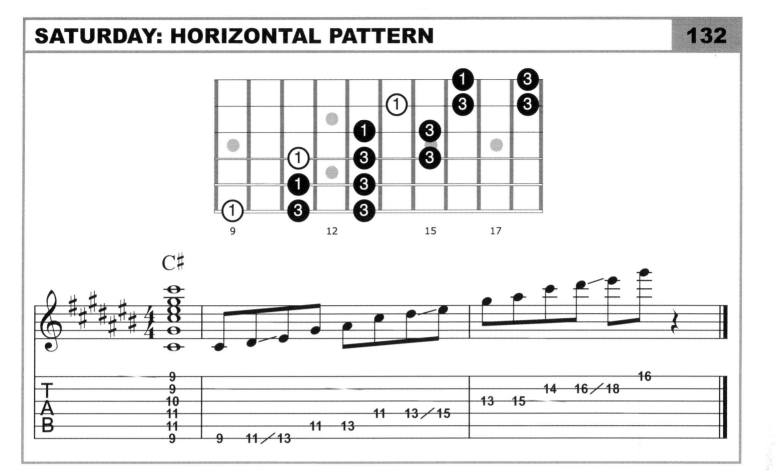

SUNDAY: SCALE APPLICATION

Groups of 4 are highly effective in the pentatonic scale, as well. Exercises like this one are great for dexterity and make great connecting phrases between ideas.

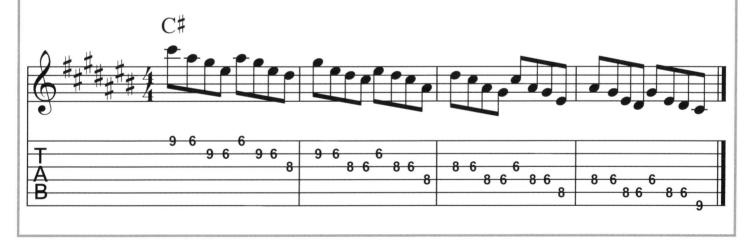

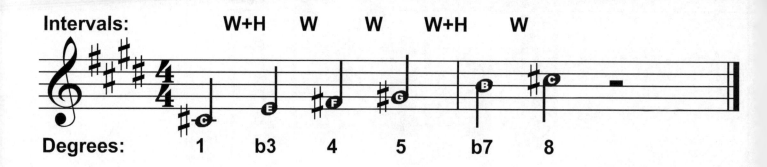

Intervals: W+H W W W+H W

Degrees: 1 b3 4 5 b7 8

MONDAY: C SHAPE | 134

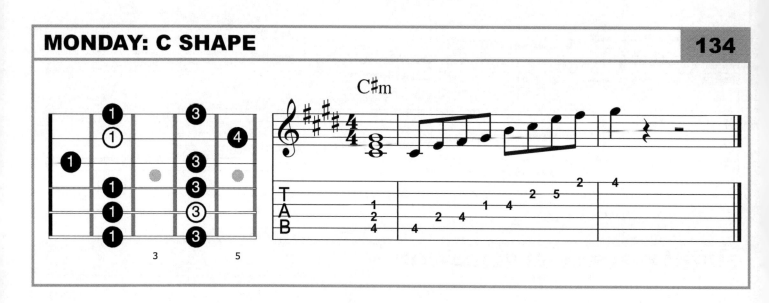

TUESDAY: A SHAPE | 135

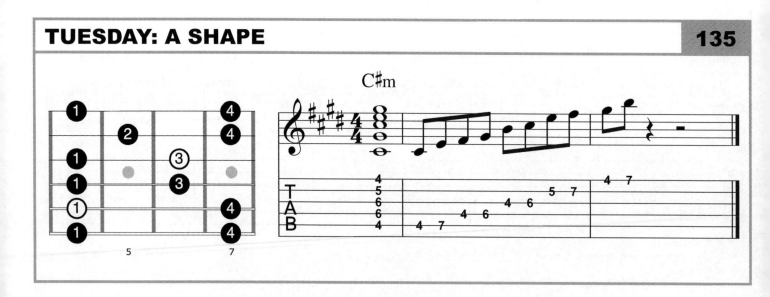

WEDNESDAY: G SHAPE

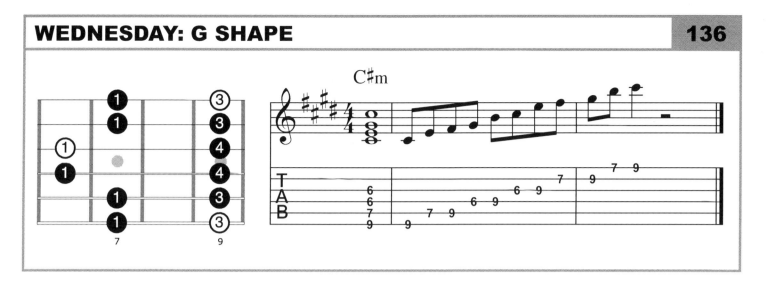

THURSDAY: E SHAPE 137

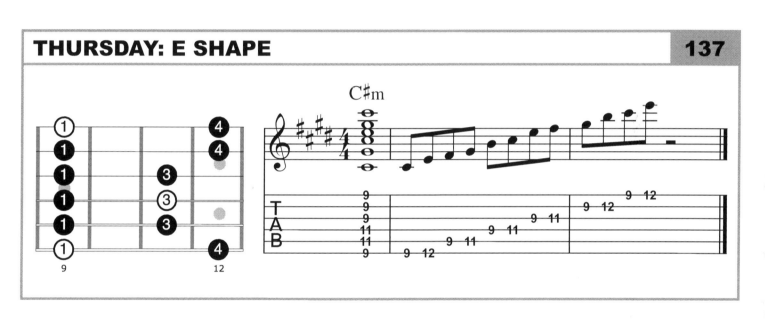

FRIDAY: D SHAPE 138

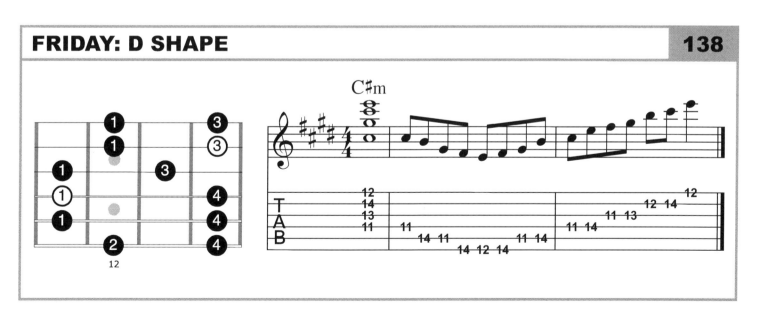

SATURDAY: HORIZONTAL PATTERN

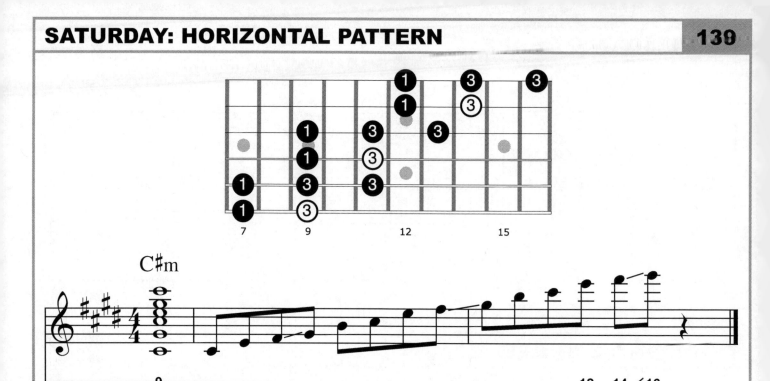

SUNDAY: SCALE APPLICATION

This week, we'll explore descending in 4s in a minor pentatonic scale. As an alternative to picking every note, you can try using a pull-off every time there are two notes on the same string. This is a great pattern to work through all the CAGED shapes for further study.

WEEK 21: D MAJOR

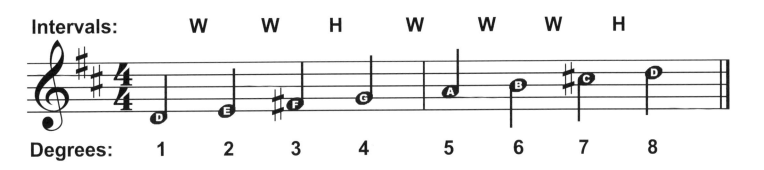

Intervals: W W H W W W H

Degrees: 1 2 3 4 5 6 7 8

MONDAY: C SHAPE | 141

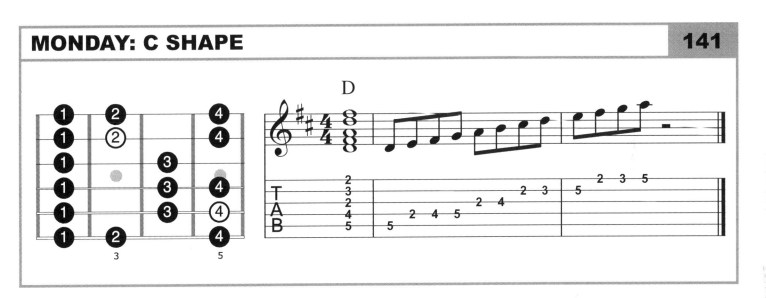

TUESDAY: A SHAPE | 142

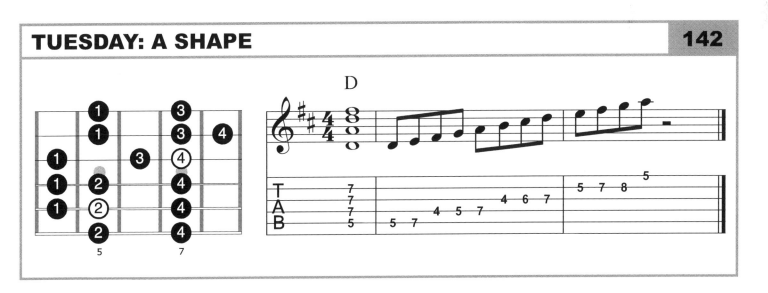

WEDNESDAY: G SHAPE

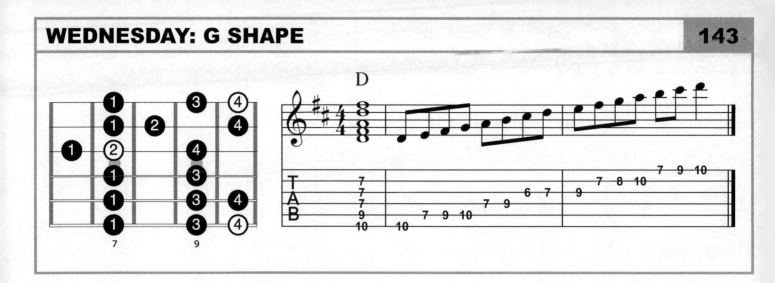

THURSDAY: E SHAPE

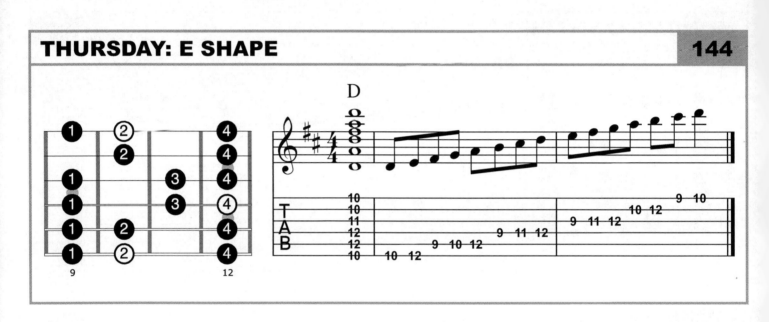

FRIDAY: D SHAPE

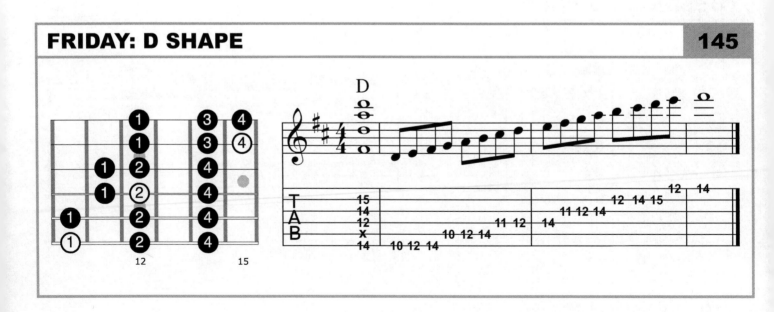

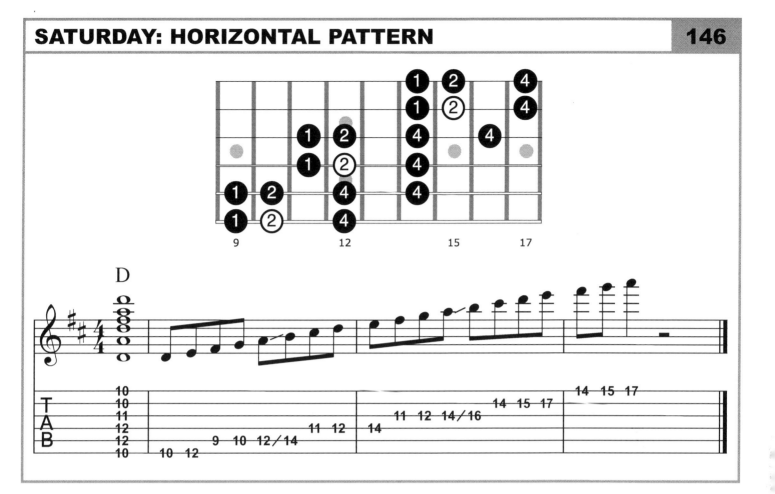

SUNDAY: SCALE APPLICATION 147

Here's a very popular scale sequence that you'll find in many melodies. It even has a distinctive look on the staff. You can think of it as descening three notes of the scale stepwise, then backing up a 3rd.

WEEK 22: D MINOR

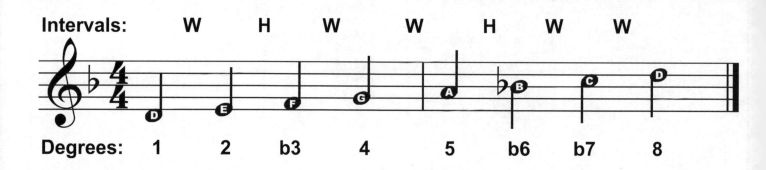

Intervals:	W	H	W	W	H	W	W
Degrees:	1	2	b3	4	5	b6	b7	8

MONDAY: C SHAPE

TUESDAY: A SHAPE

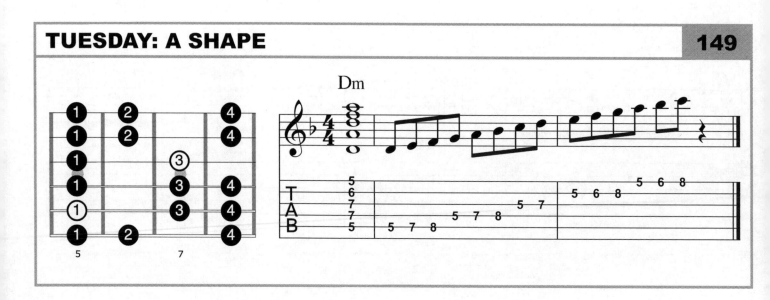

WEDNESDAY: G SHAPE

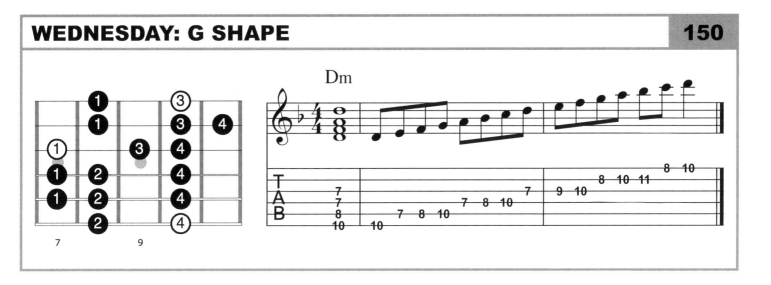

THURSDAY: E SHAPE

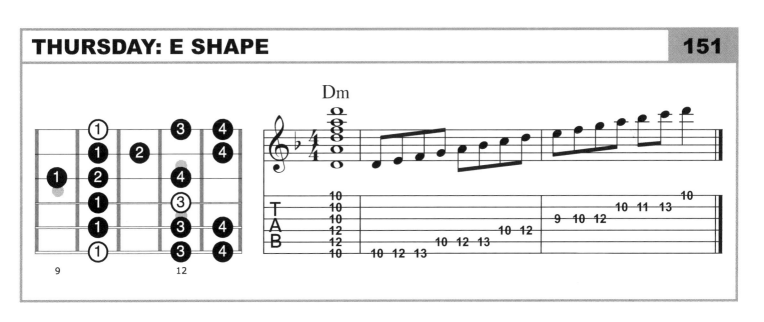

FRIDAY: D SHAPE

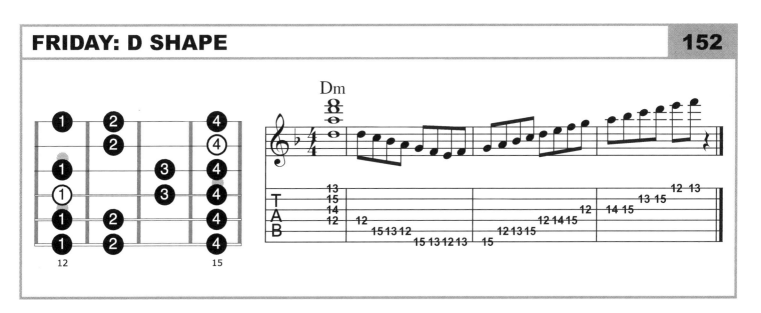

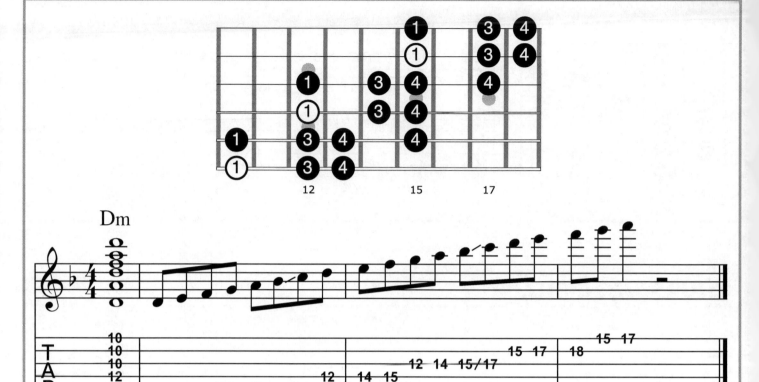

Like major chords, melodies resolve to chord tones over minor chords: a 2nd will resolve to the root or 3rd, a 4th will resolve to a 3rd or 5th, a 6th will resolve to a 5th or climb up to the root, and a 7th will resolve to the root or fall to the 5th. Let's explore this in the A Shape.

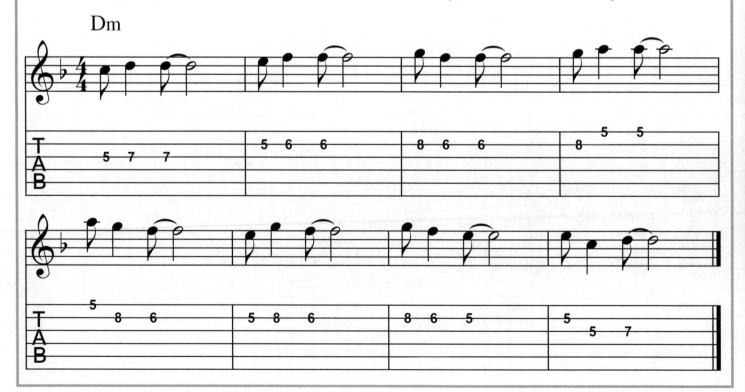

WEEK 23: D MAJOR PENTATONIC

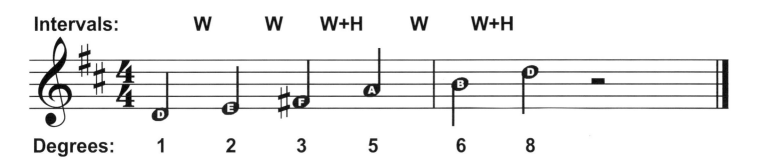

Intervals: W W W+H W W+H
Degrees: 1 2 3 5 6 8

MONDAY: C SHAPE   155

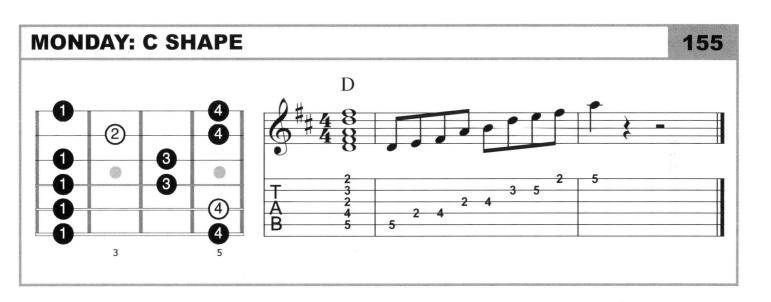

TUESDAY: A SHAPE   156

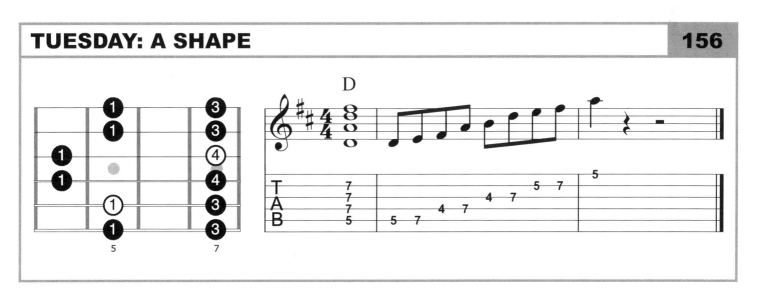

WEDNESDAY: G SHAPE

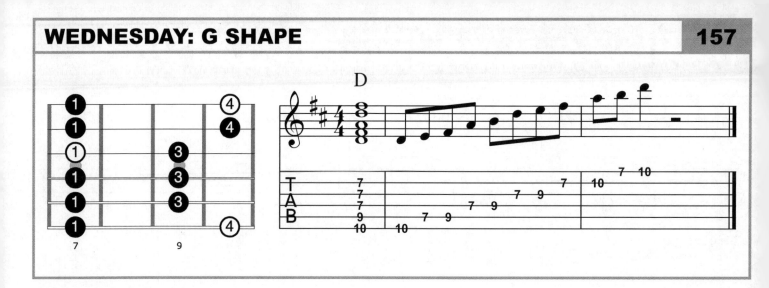

THURSDAY: E SHAPE

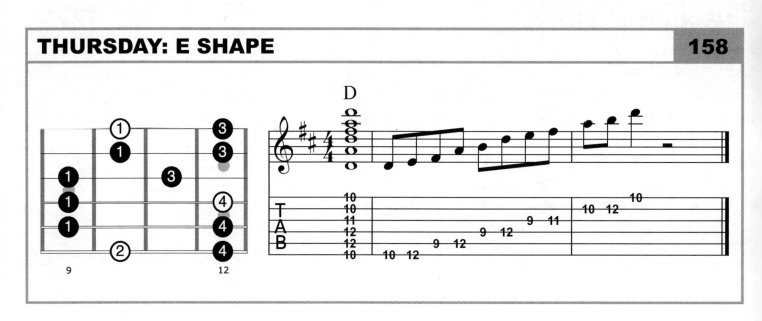

FRIDAY: D SHAPE

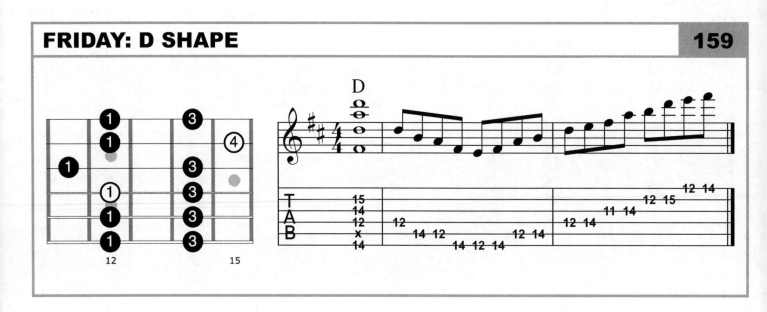

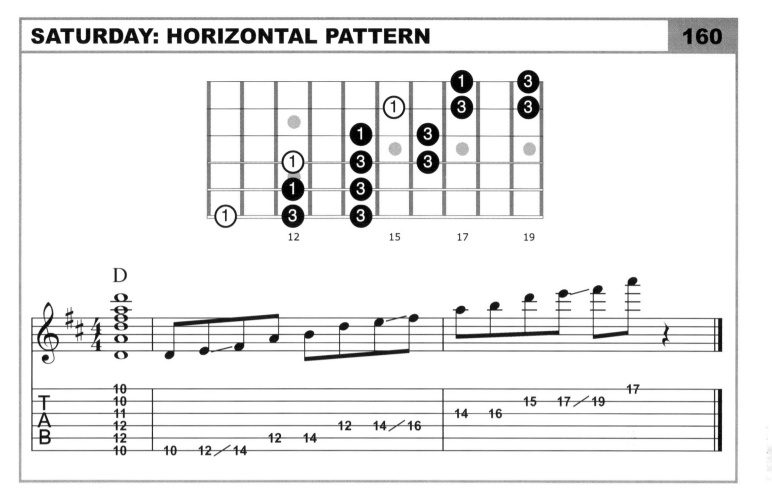

Ascending in 4s is another highly useful way to build excitement while connecting phrases.

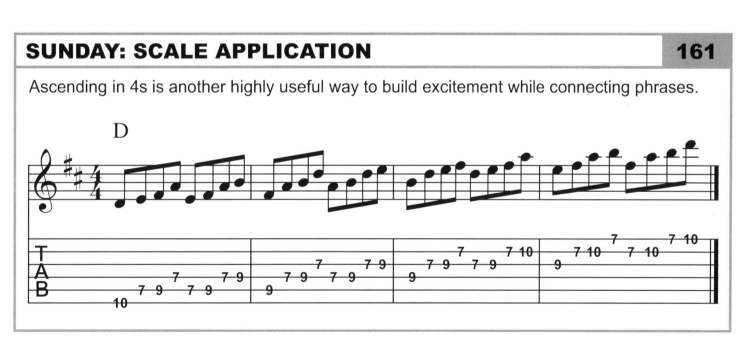

WEEK 24: D MINOR PENTATONIC

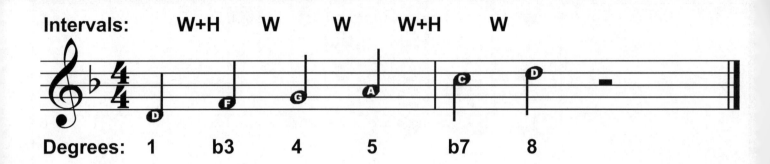

Intervals:		W+H		W		W		W+H		W	
Degrees:	1		b3		4		5		b7	8	

MONDAY: C SHAPE   162

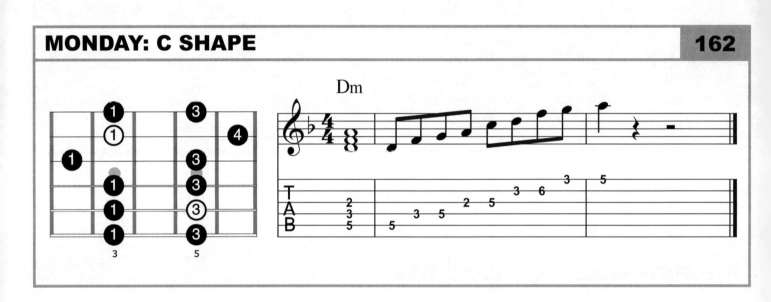

TUESDAY: A SHAPE   163

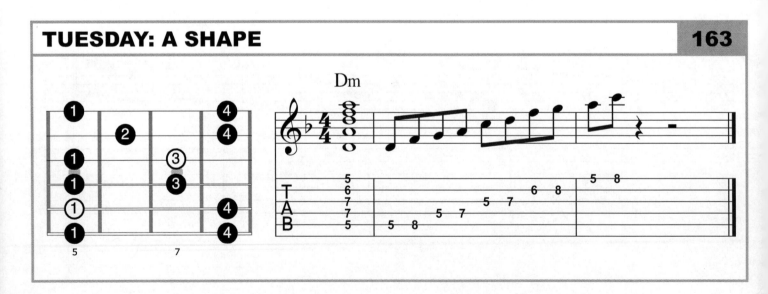

WEDNESDAY: G SHAPE

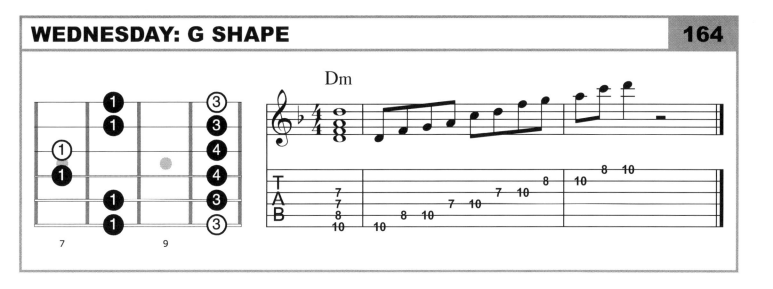

THURSDAY: E SHAPE

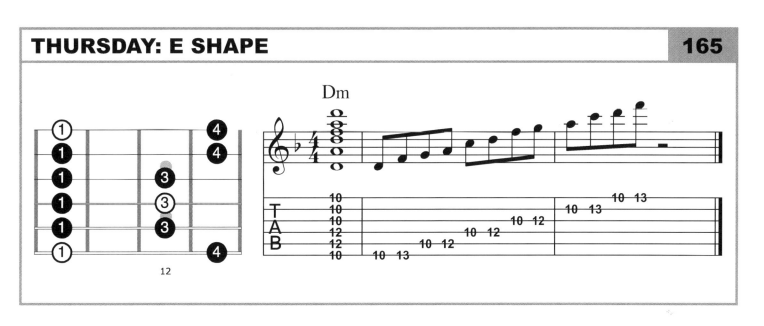

FRIDAY: D SHAPE

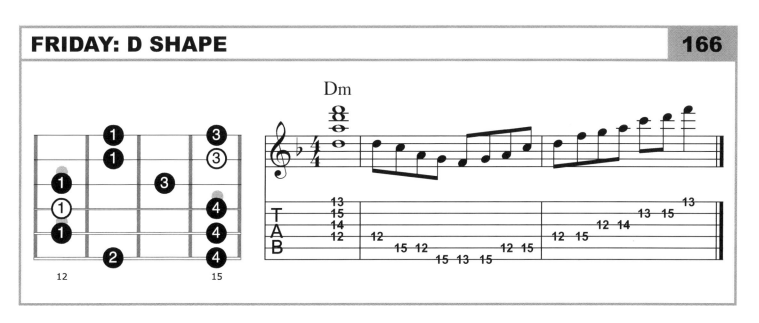

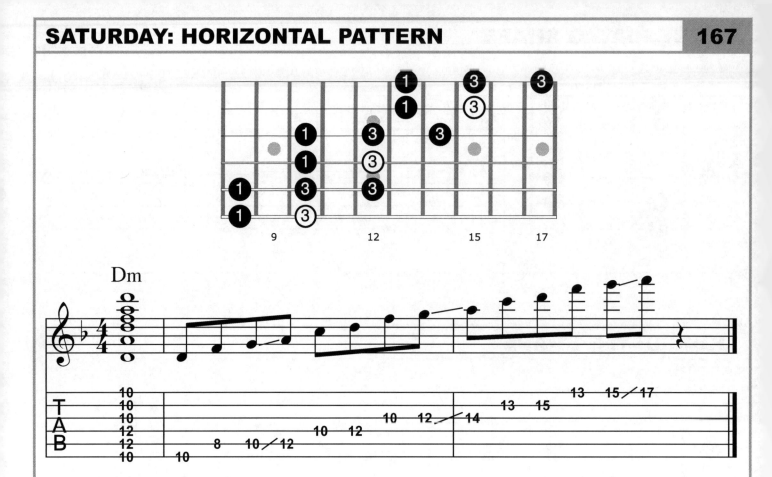

SUNDAY: SCALE APPLICATION

Ascending 4s within the minor pentatonic yields great results, as well! This example really demonstrates how the starting and ending notes of the fingering pattern affect the sound of the scale.

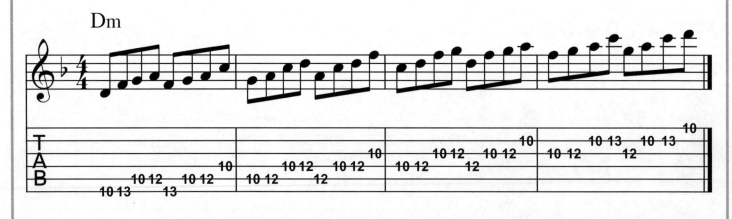

WEEK 25: E♭ MAJOR

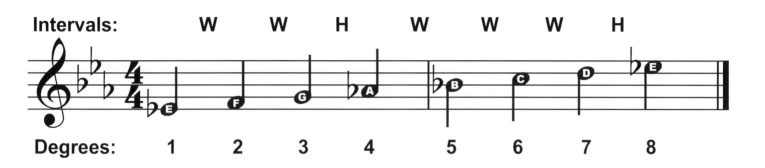

Intervals:	W	W	H	W	W	W	H

Degrees: 1   2   3   4   5   6   7   8

MONDAY: C SHAPE   169

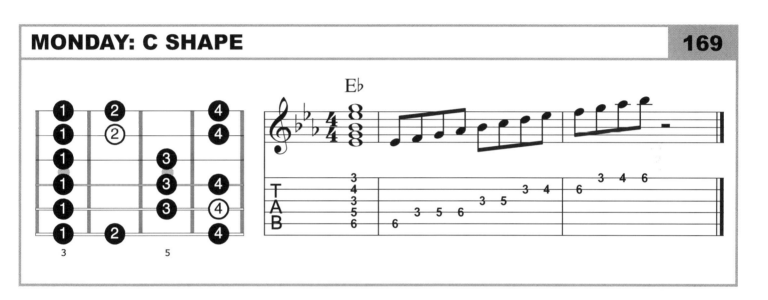

TUESDAY: A SHAPE   170

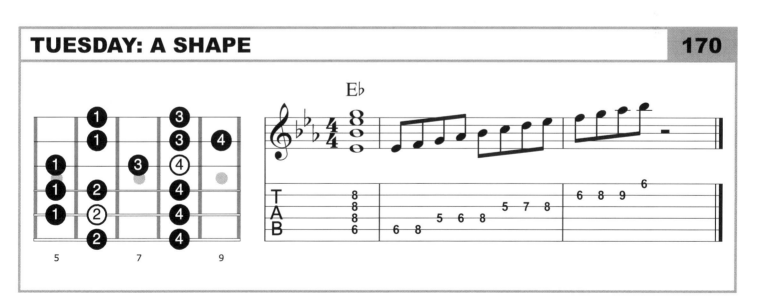

WEDNESDAY: G SHAPE

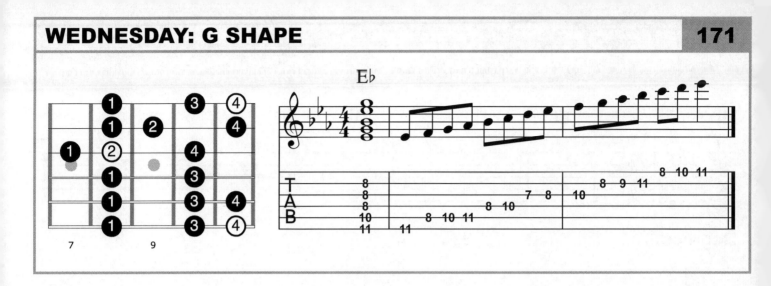

THURSDAY: E SHAPE
172

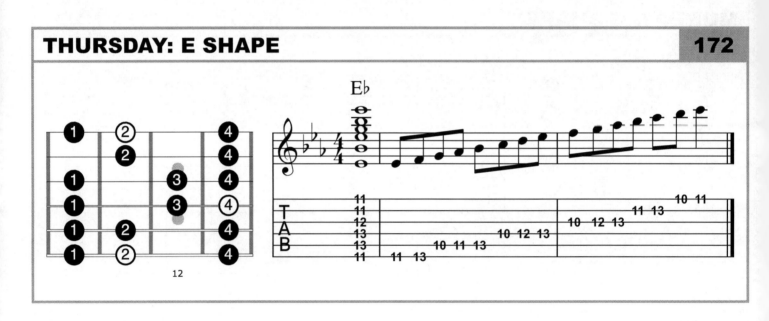

FRIDAY: D SHAPE
173

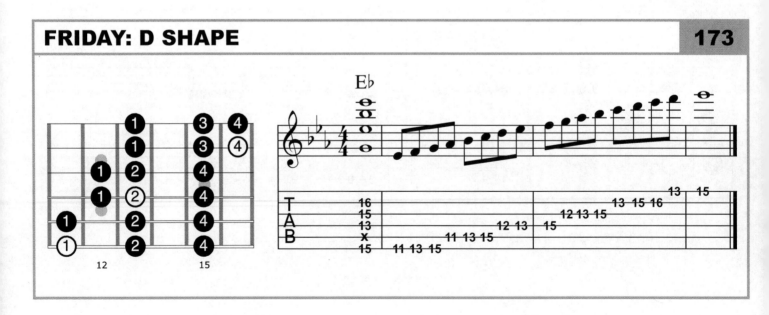

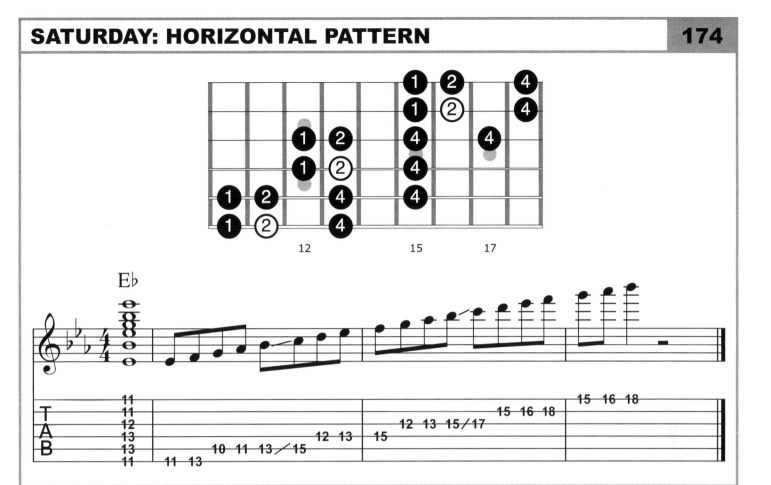

Our next melody uses the A Shape. It combines shifting an idea to a new set of strings and resolving on chord tones.

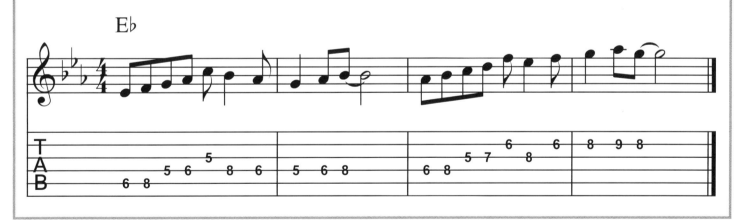

WEEK 26: E♭ MINOR

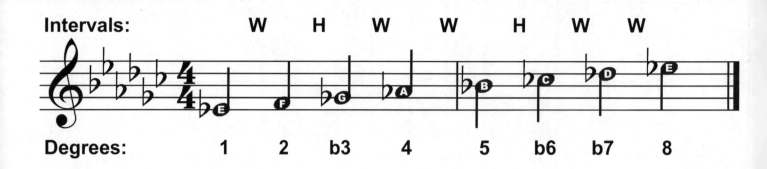

Intervals:		W		H		W		W		H		W		W	
Degrees:		1		2		b3		4		5		b6		b7		8

MONDAY: D SHAPE

176

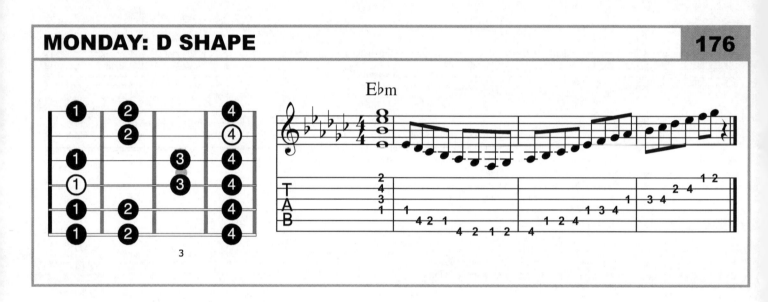

TUESDAY: C SHAPE

177

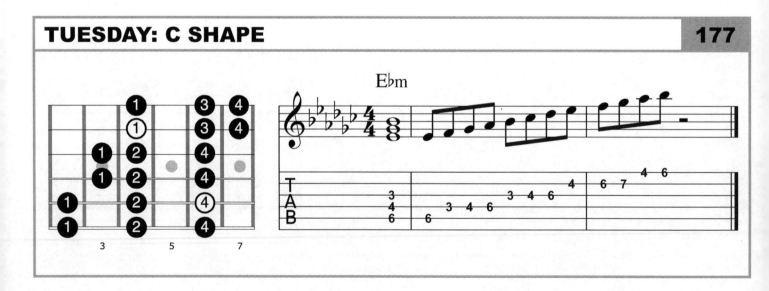

84

WEDNESDAY: A SHAPE

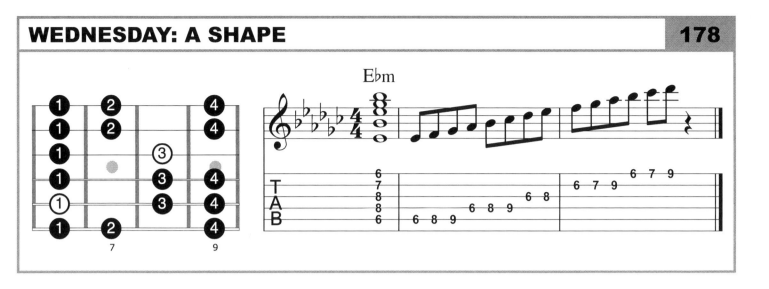

THURSDAY: G SHAPE

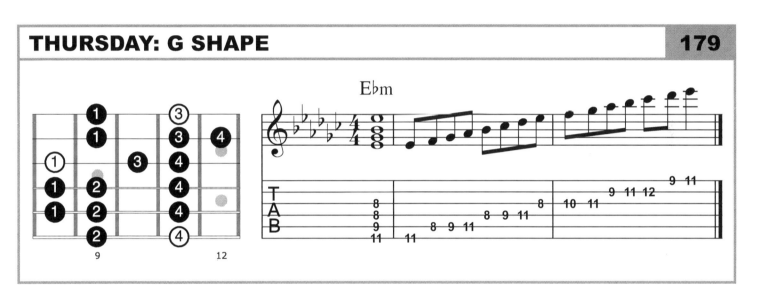

FRIDAY: E SHAPE

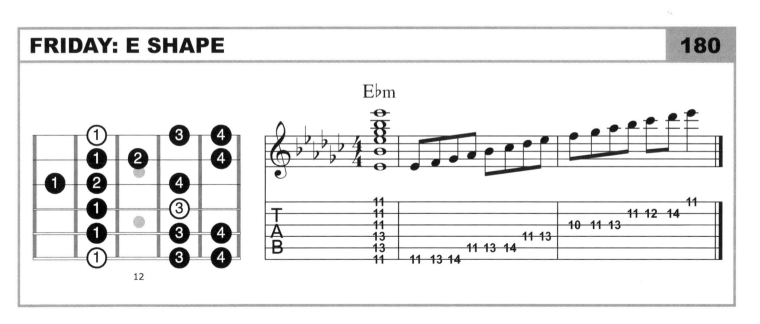

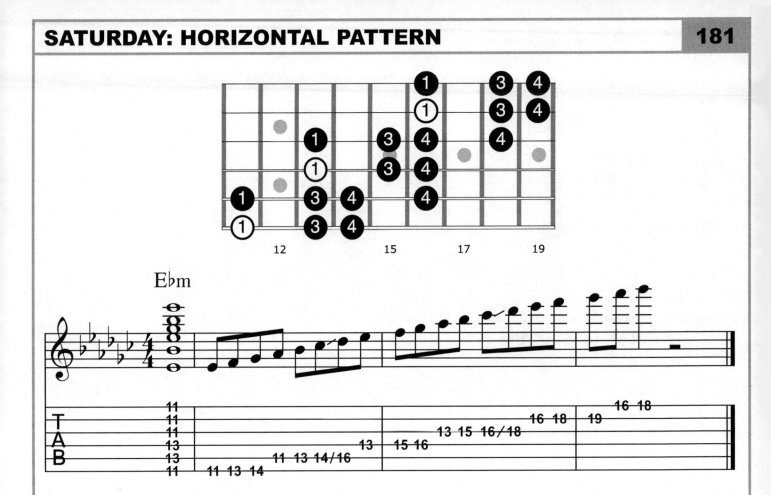

Our next example is a common variation of the scale sequence presented in Week 21. It uses the G Shape and involves descending by a 3rd interval, then ascending three notes stepwise.

WEEK 27: E♭ MAJOR PENTATONIC

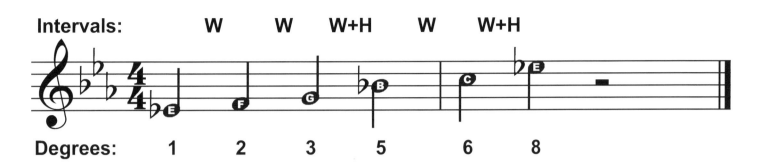

Intervals:		W	W	W+H	W	W+H
Degrees:	1	2	3	5	6	8

MONDAY: C SHAPE

183

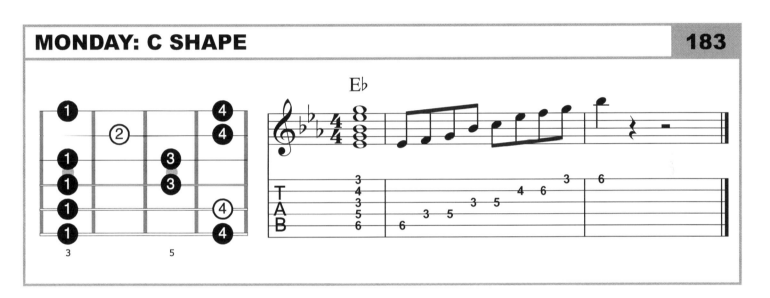

TUESDAY: A SHAPE

184

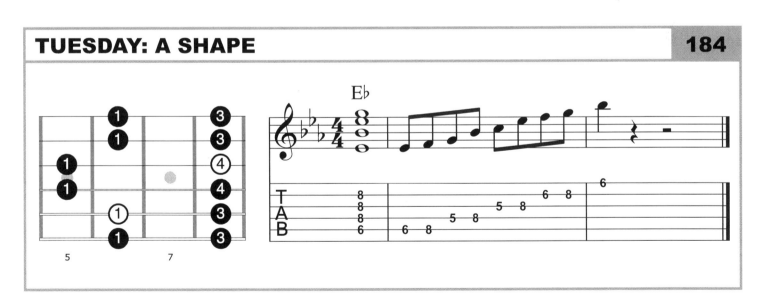

WEDNESDAY: G SHAPE

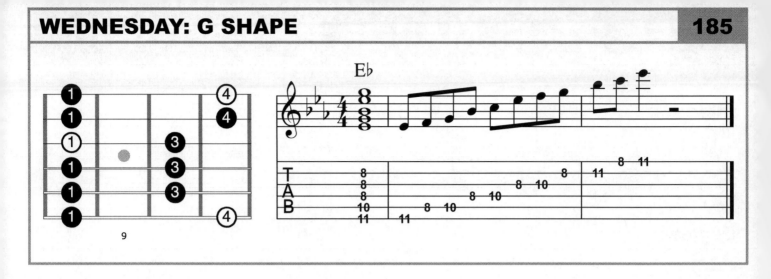

THURSDAY: E SHAPE

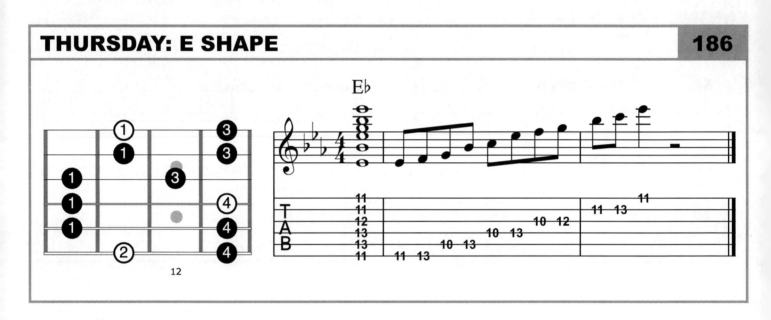

FRIDAY: D SHAPE

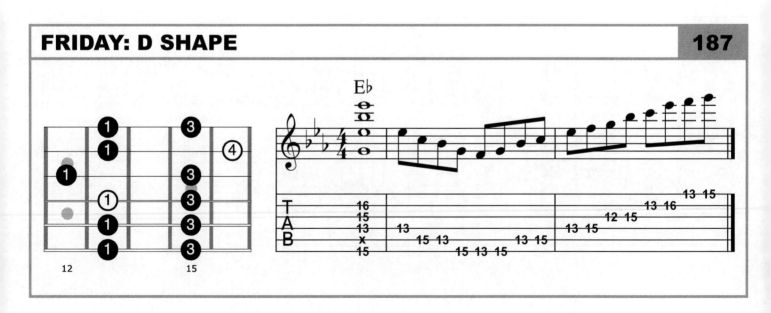

SATURDAY: HORIZONTAL PATTERN

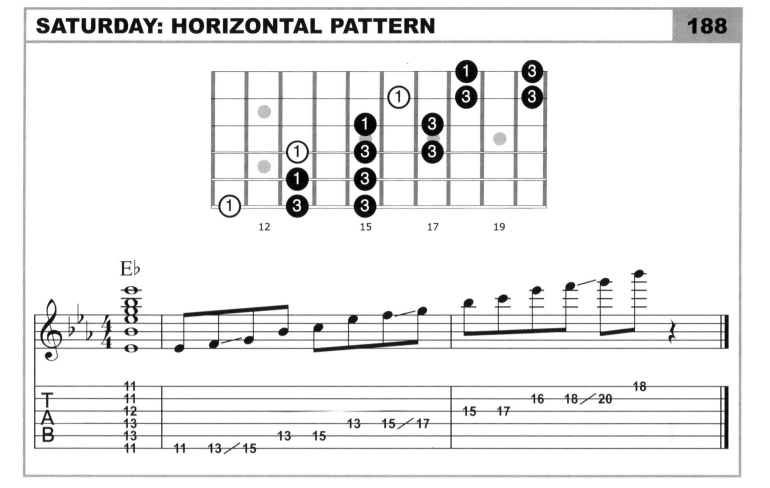

SUNDAY: SCALE APPLICATION

New rhythm patterns are a great way to spice up your scale passages. A common rhythmic device is to play a measure of 8th notes grouped as 123–123–12. This phrase uses the E Shape and the descending 3s pattern with two stepwise notes ascending at the end. It also moves the pattern across strings. Try each measure separately to get started, then play the entire pattern.

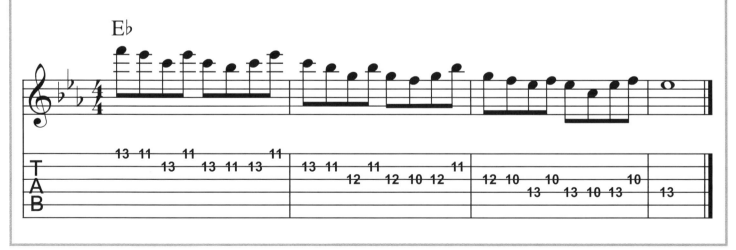

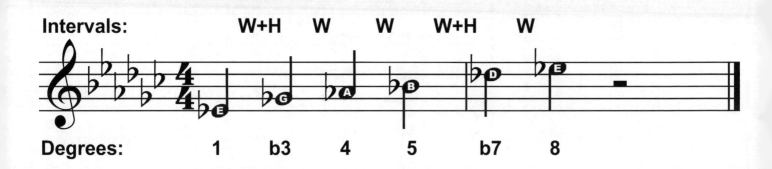

Intervals: W+H   W   W   W+H   W

Degrees: 1   b3   4   5   b7   8

MONDAY: D SHAPE   190

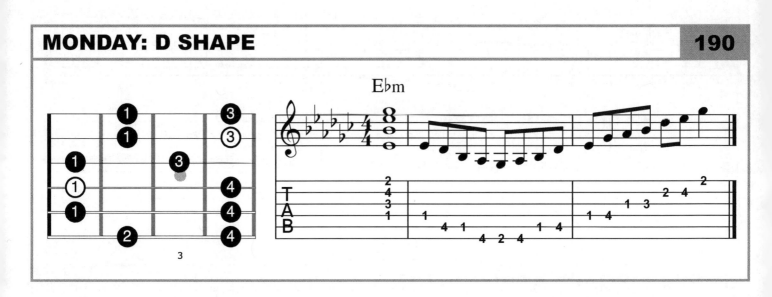

TUESDAY: C SHAPE   191

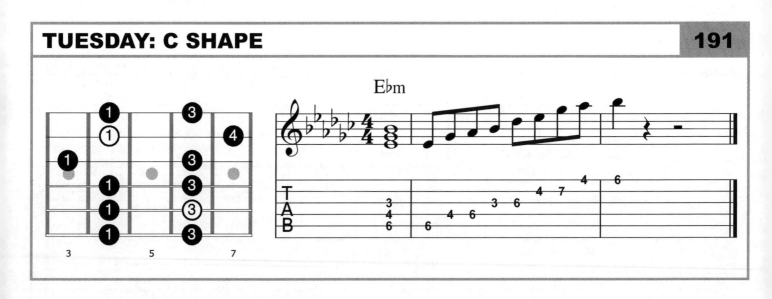

WEDNESDAY: A SHAPE

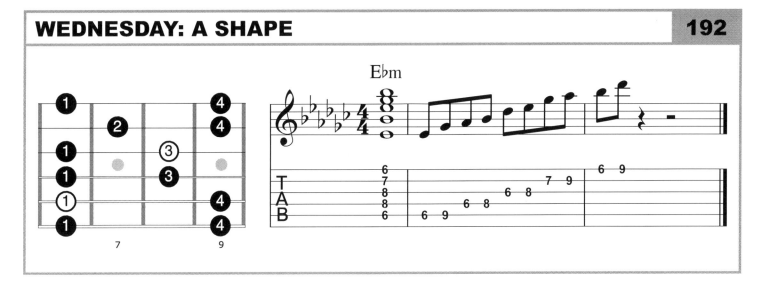

THURSDAY: G SHAPE

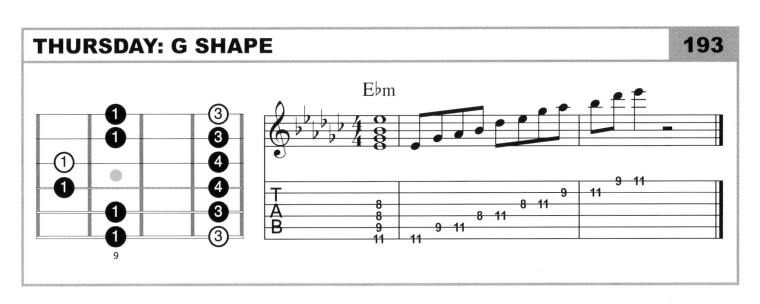

FRIDAY: E SHAPE

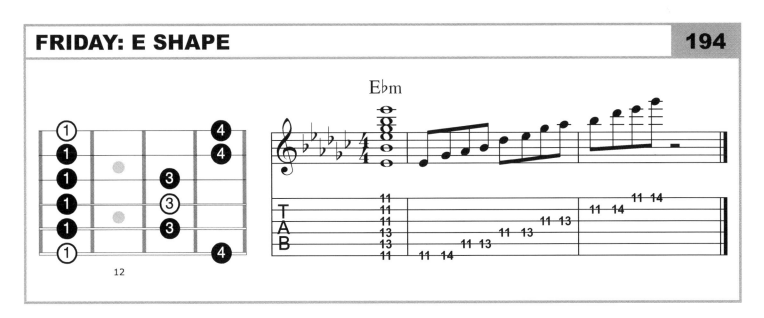

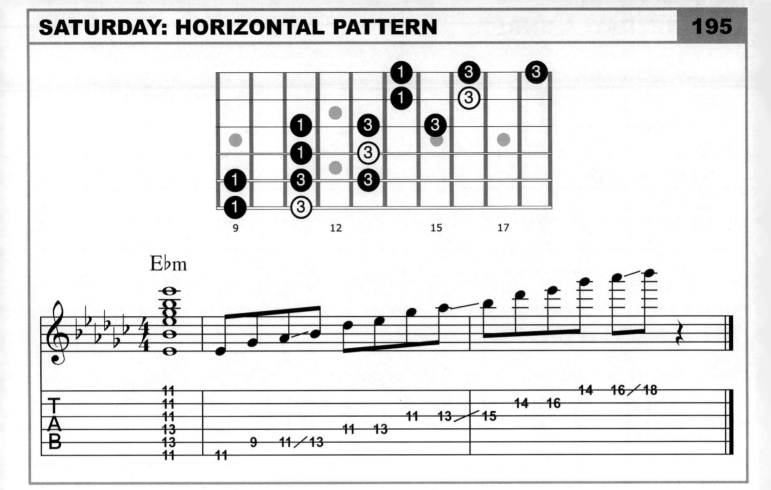

Our next pattern is essentially reversing the direction of last Sunday's exercise. We'll ascend in 3s twice, then descend two notes stepwise to create our 123–123–12 rhythm pattern. Once you internalize the pattern, you can move it to any pair of strings within the pentatonic scale, in any of the CAGED patterns.

WEEK 29: E MAJOR

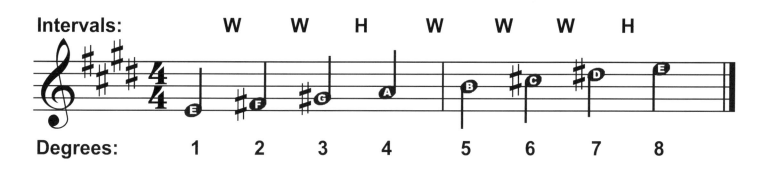

MONDAY: C SHAPE — 197

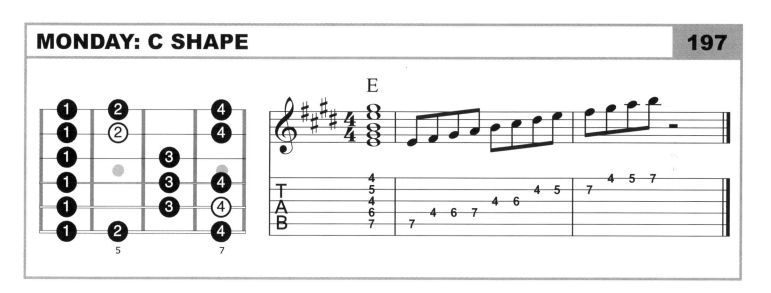

TUESDAY: A SHAPE — 198

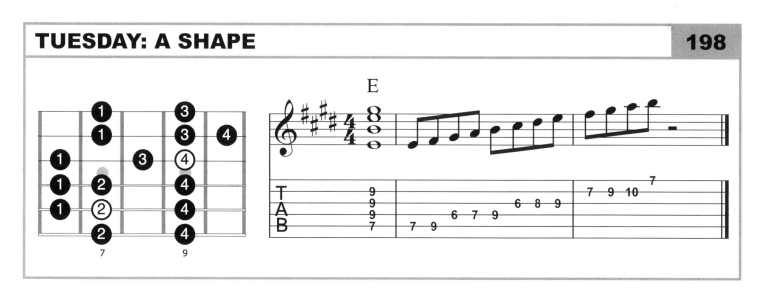

WEDNESDAY: G SHAPE

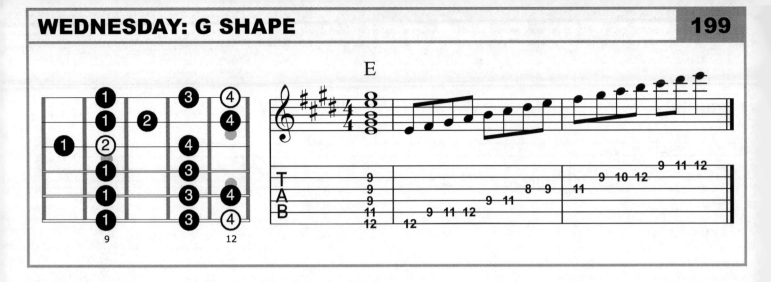

THURSDAY: E SHAPE

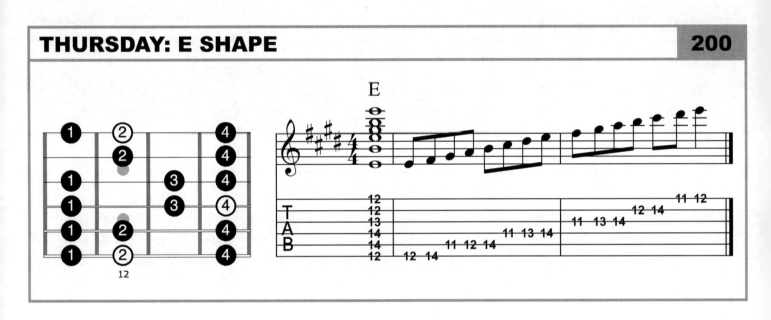

FRIDAY: D SHAPE

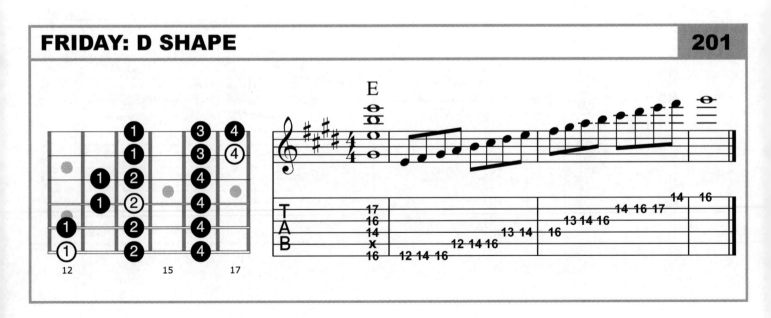

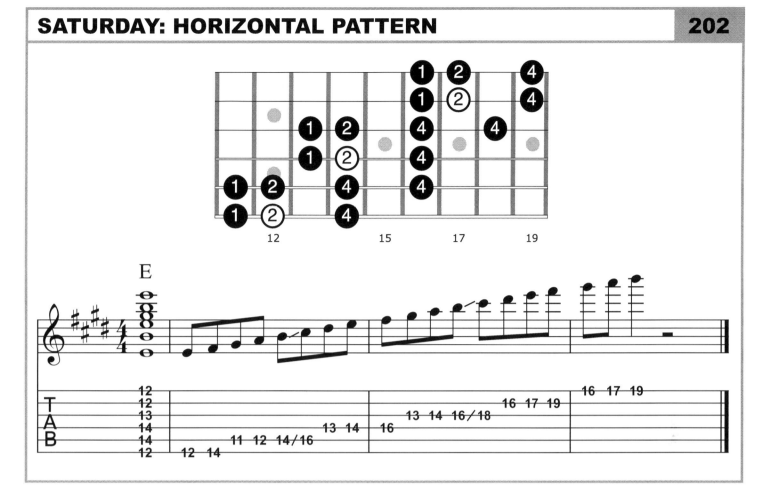

Another scale sequence you'll find in many melodies is a variation of Week 26. You can think of this pattern as three notes ascending stepwise and one note descending by a 3rd.

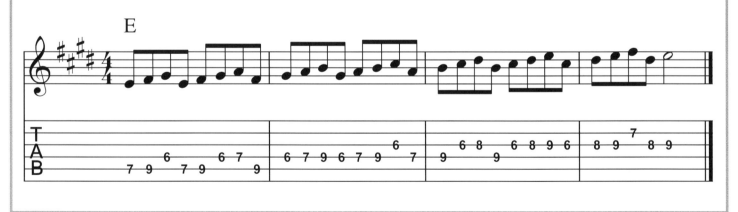

WEEK 30: E MINOR

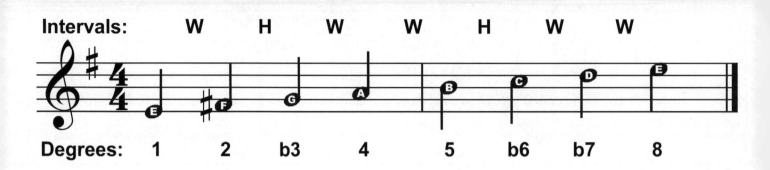

Intervals:	W	H	W	W	H	W	W

Degrees: 1   2   b3   4   5   b6   b7   8

MONDAY: D SHAPE   204

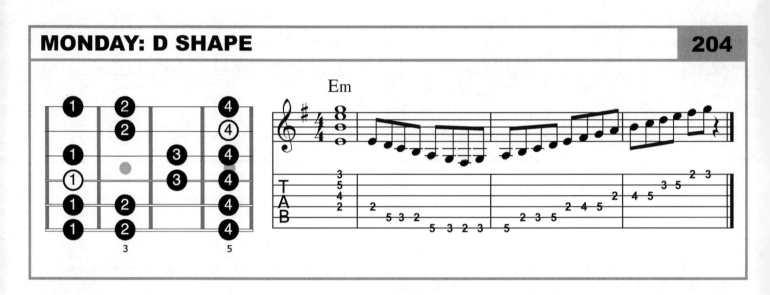

TUESDAY: C SHAPE   205

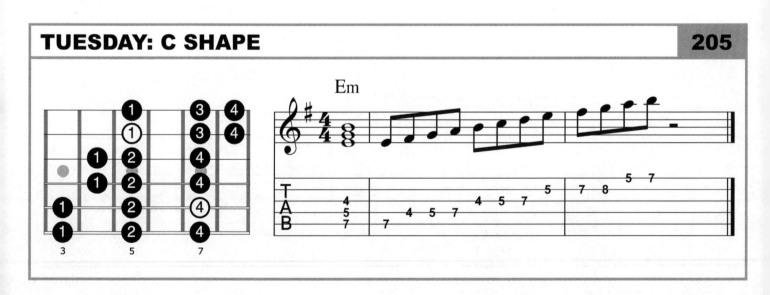

WEDNESDAY: A SHAPE

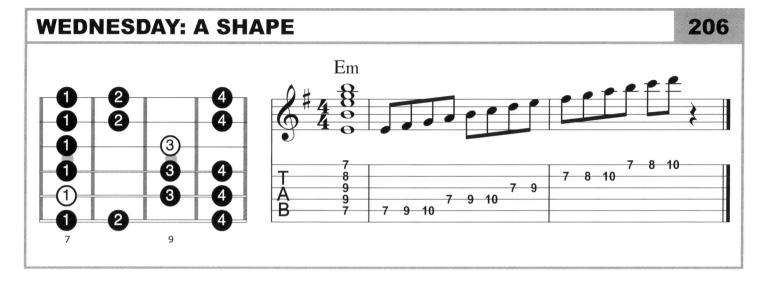

THURSDAY: G SHAPE

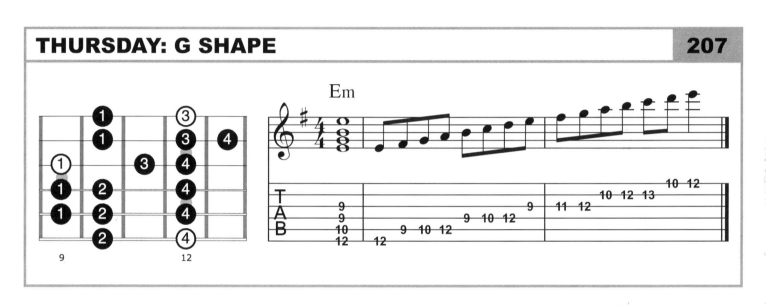

FRIDAY: E SHAPE

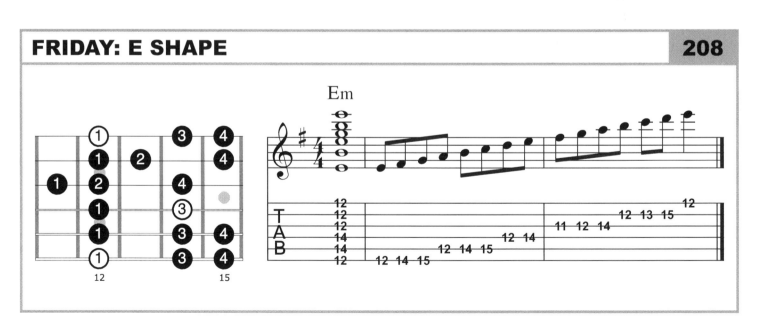

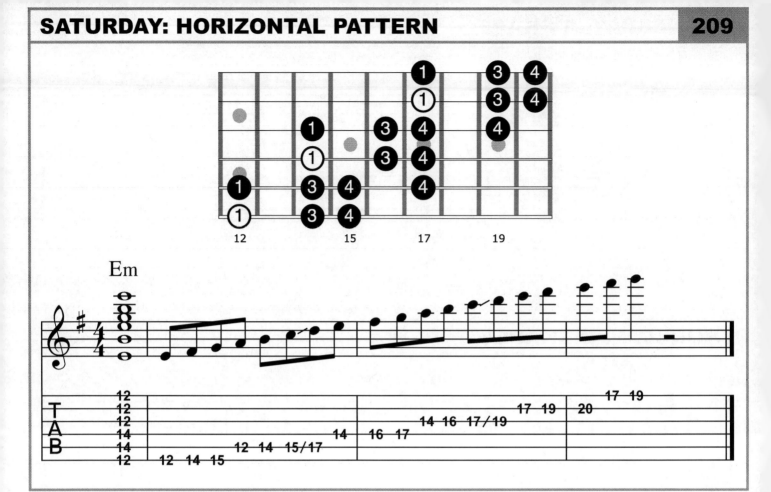

This scale sequence uses the D Shape and is a variation of Week 21's application. You can think of it as ascending by a 3rd and then descening three notes stepwise.

WEEK 31: E MAJOR PENTATONIC

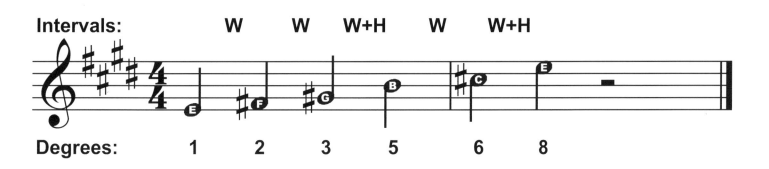

Intervals: W W W+H W W+H

Degrees: 1 2 3 5 6 8

MONDAY: D SHAPE 211

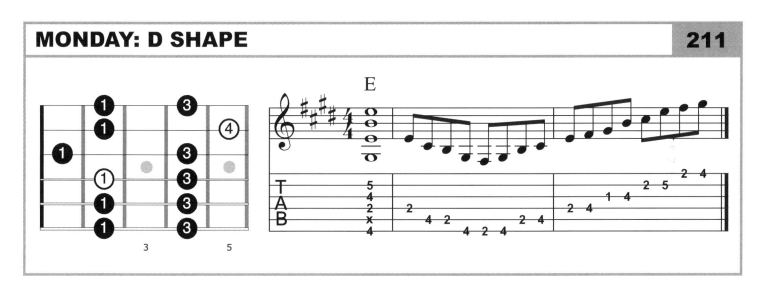

TUESDAY: C SHAPE 212

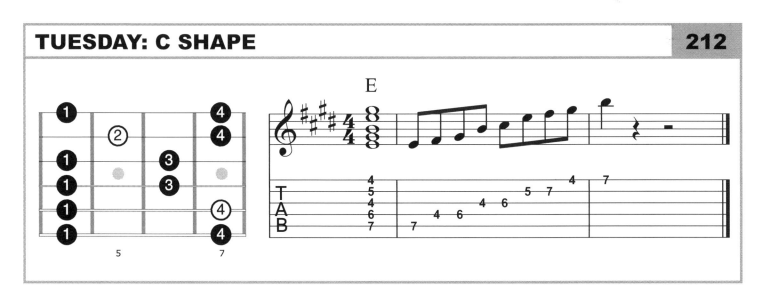

WEDNESDAY: A SHAPE

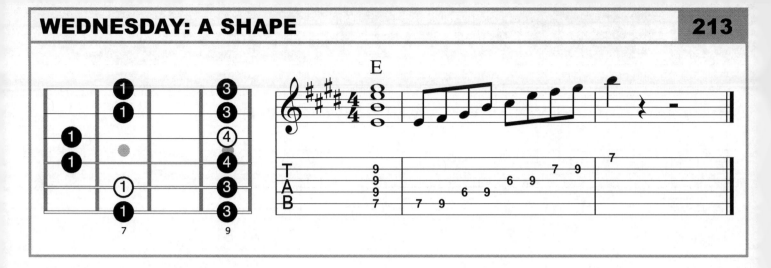

THURSDAY: G SHAPE

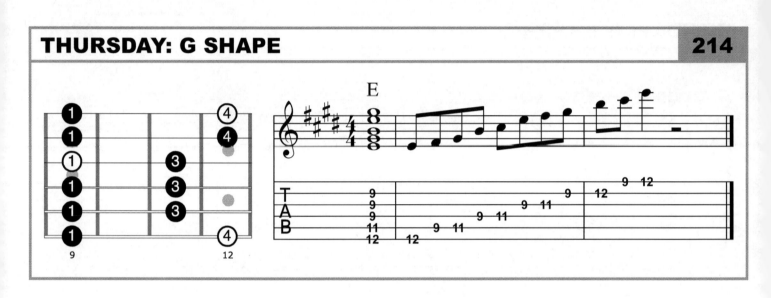

FRIDAY: E SHAPE

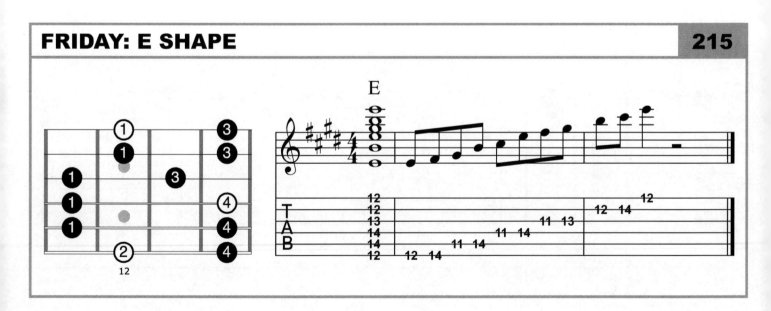

SATURDAY: HORIZONTAL PATTERN

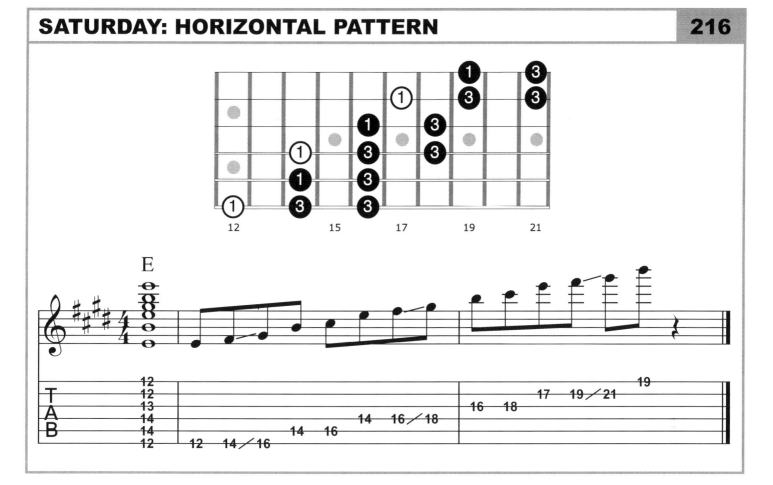

SUNDAY: SCALE APPLICATION

The melody below is an example of combining phrases and sequences you have already learned. It uses ascending 4s, rolling a finger, and moving an idea across strings to continue a musical idea.

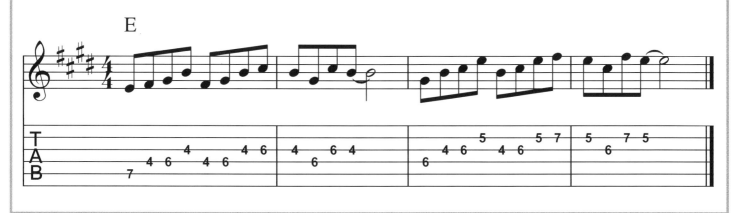

WEEK 32: E MINOR PENTATONIC

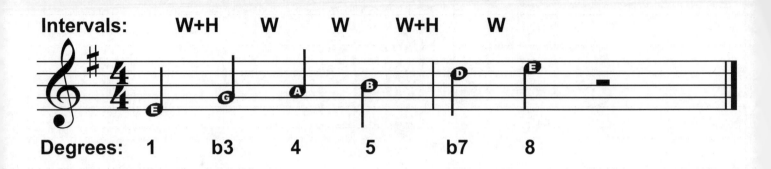

Intervals: W+H W W W+H W

Degrees: 1 b3 4 5 b7 8

MONDAY: D SHAPE
218

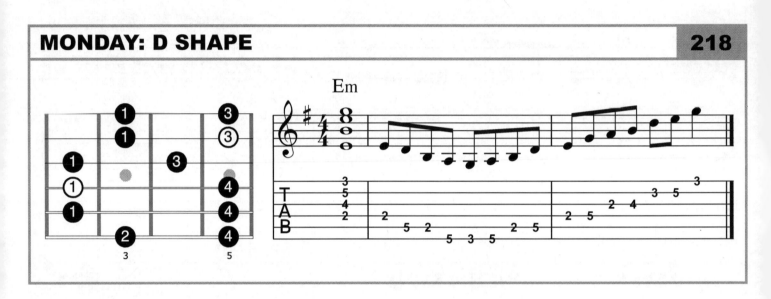

TUESDAY: C SHAPE
219

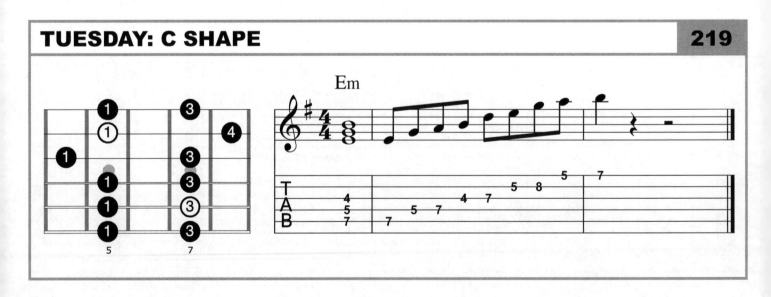

WEDNESDAY: A SHAPE

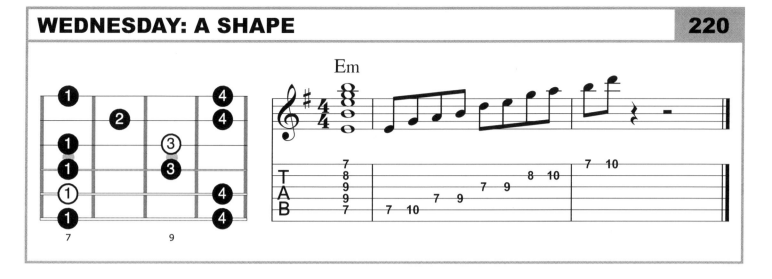

THURSDAY: G SHAPE

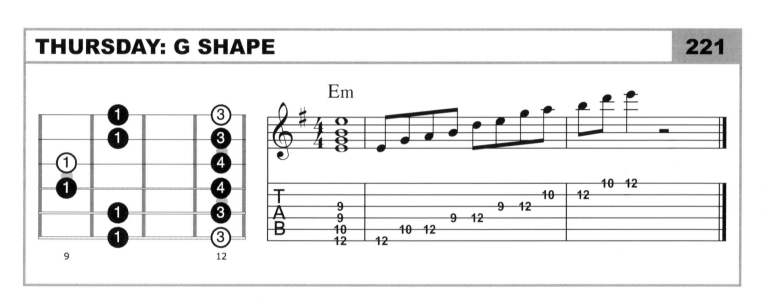

FRIDAY: E SHAPE

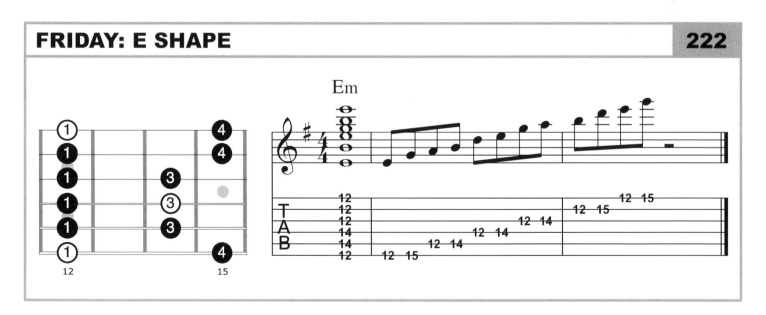

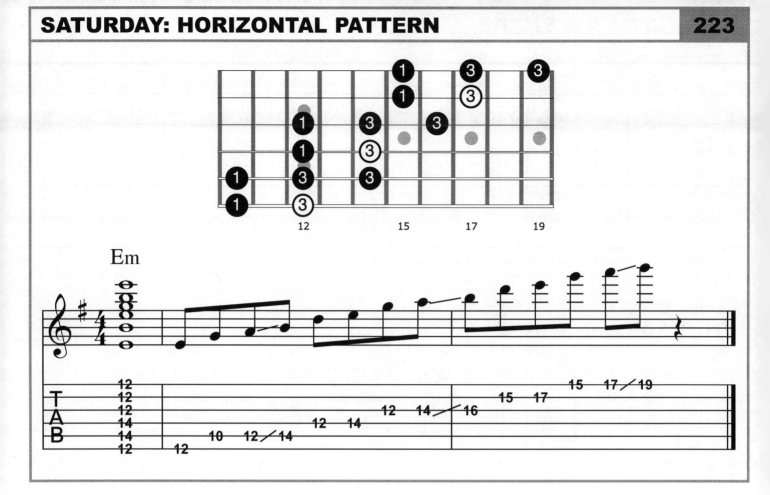

This example combines ascending and descending groups of 3 in a strict triplet rhythm. It uses the G Shape and makes for a great connecting phrase, as well as a standalone musical idea.

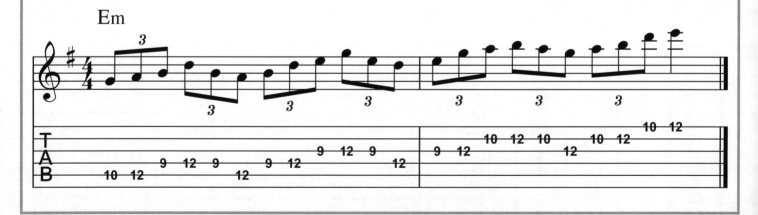

WEEK 33: F MAJOR

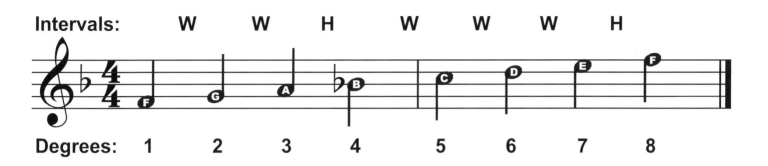

Intervals:	W	W	H	W	W	W	H

F G A B♭ C D E F

Degrees:	1	2	3	4	5	6	7	8

MONDAY: D SHAPE 225

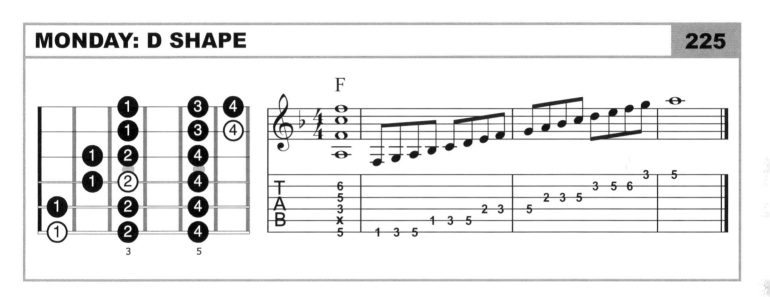

TUESDAY: C SHAPE 226

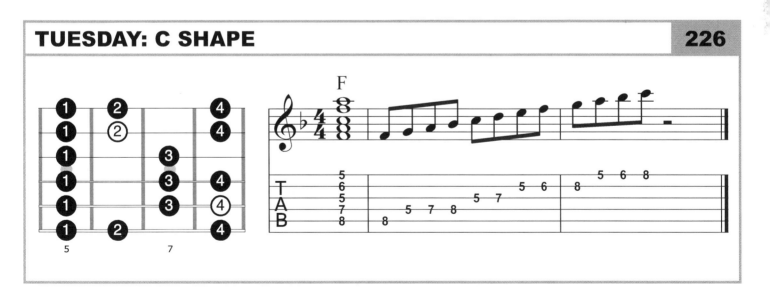

WEDNESDAY: A SHAPE

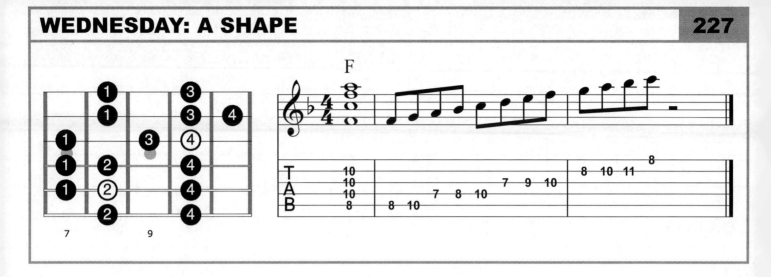

THURSDAY: G SHAPE

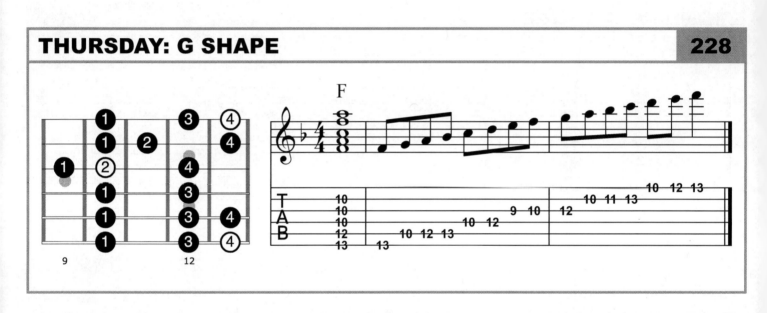

FRIDAY: E SHAPE

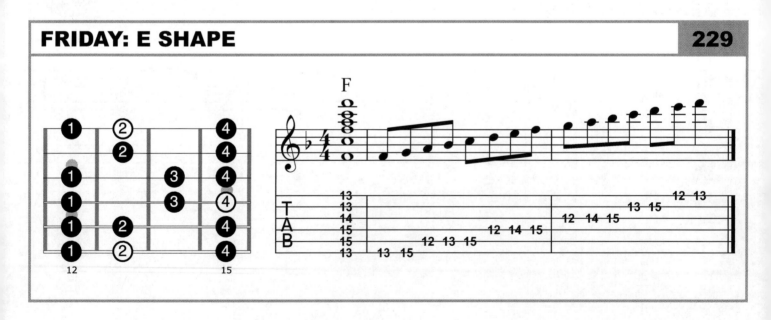

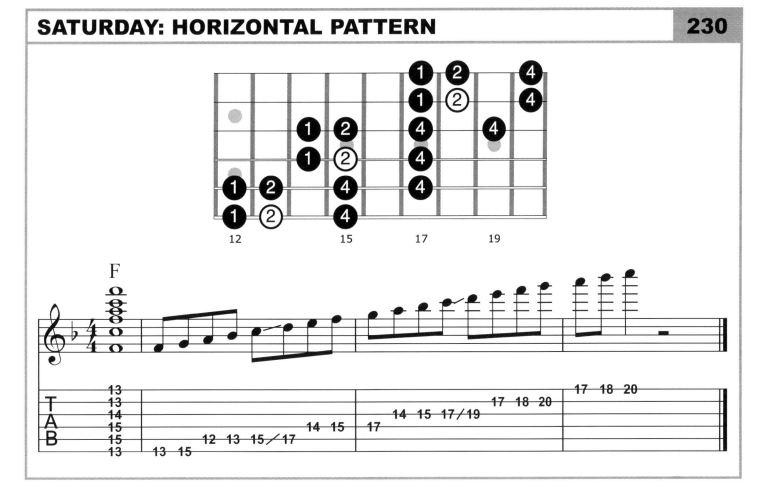

SUNDAY: SCALE APPLICATION 231

Since the major pentatonic scale is just the major scale without the 4th and 7th scale degrees, both scales can be used over a chord progression in the key of F. Many melodies switch back and forth between each scale's sound. Try to spot where this occurs in the following example.

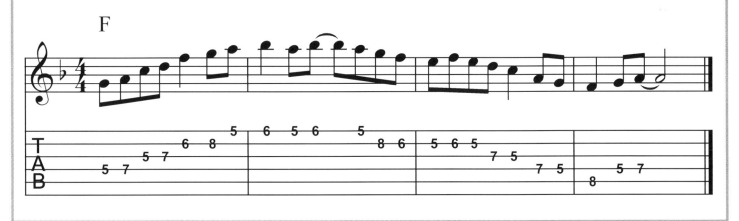

WEEK 34: F MINOR

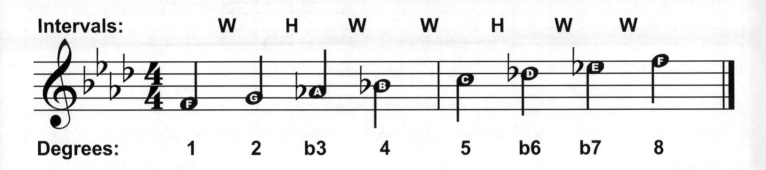

Intervals:		W		H		W		W		H		W		W	
Degrees:	1	2	b3	4	5	b6	b7	8

MONDAY: D SHAPE   232

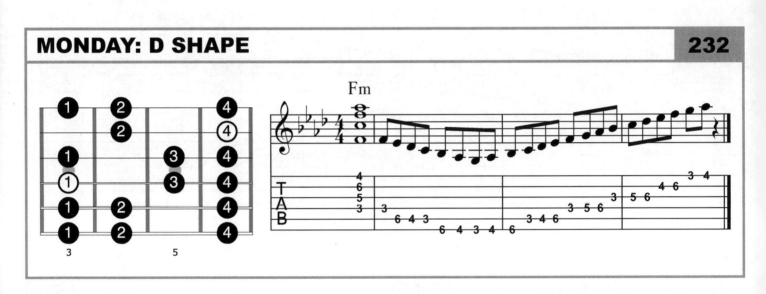

TUESDAY: C SHAPE   233

108

WEDNESDAY: A SHAPE

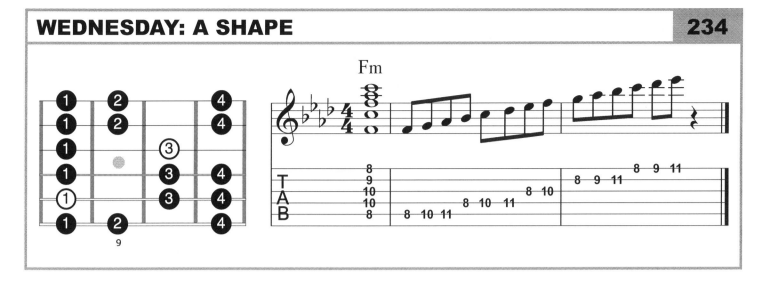

THURSDAY: G SHAPE

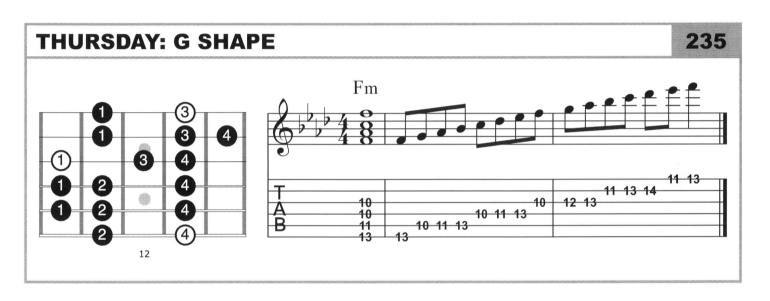

FRIDAY: E SHAPE

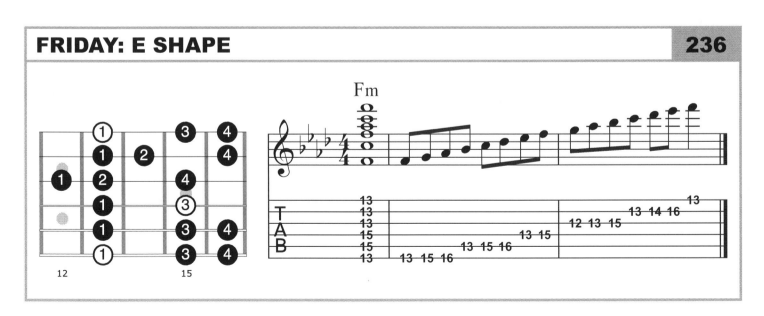

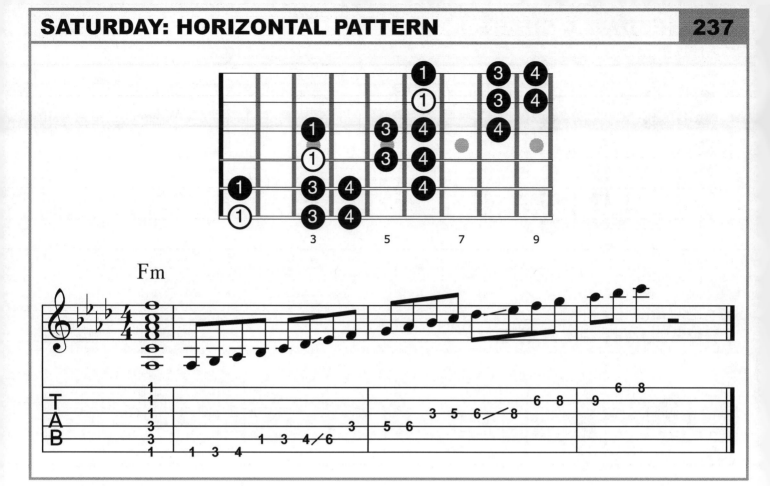

As with the major example last week, the minor pentatonic scale is simply the minor scale minus two notes (2nd and ♭6th). Spot where the melody shifts between the two scales in this C-Shape example.

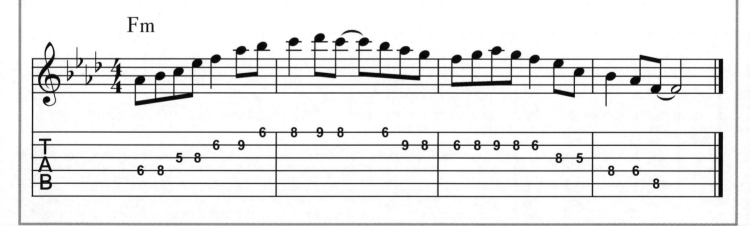

WEEK 35: F MAJOR PENTATONIC

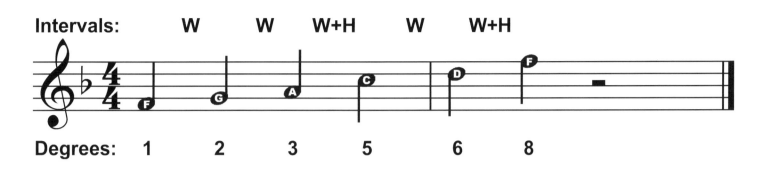

Intervals:		W	W	W+H	W	W+H

Degrees: 1 2 3 5 6 8

MONDAY: D SHAPE 239

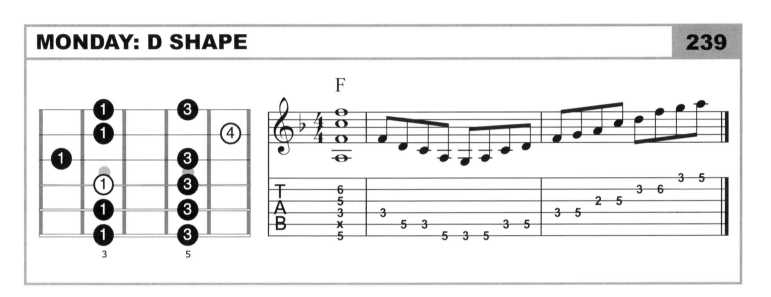

TUESDAY: C SHAPE 240

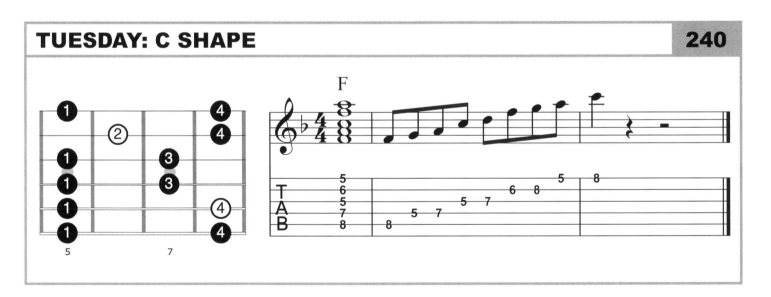

WEDNESDAY: A SHAPE

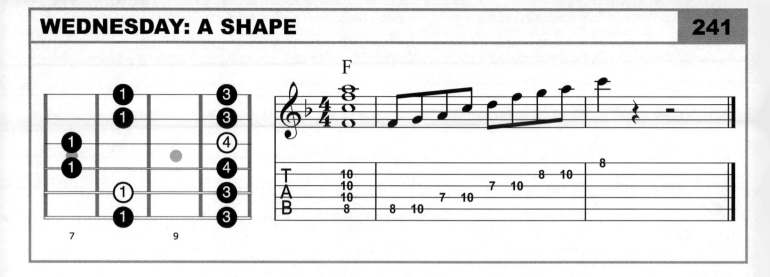

THURSDAY: G SHAPE

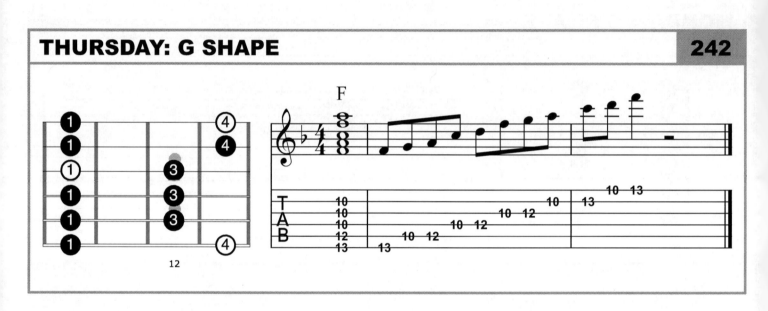

FRIDAY: E SHAPE

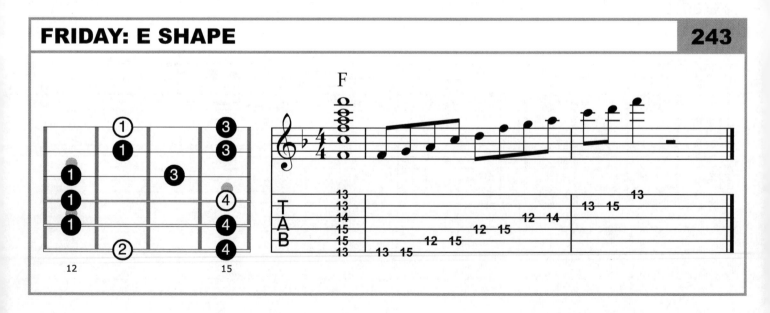

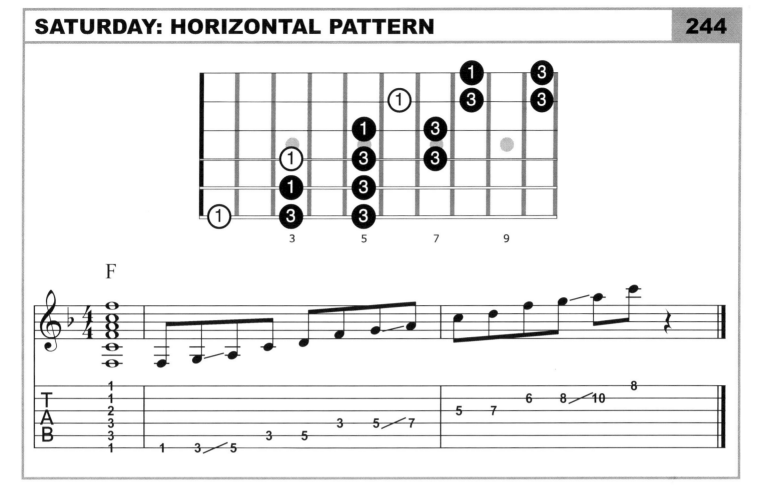

Another common way guitarists descend in 4s is to move a pattern to a different set of strings. In the example below, the half note gives the listener a break while creating an ending to the phrase. For additional study, you can try using a pull-off to articulate each pair of notes.

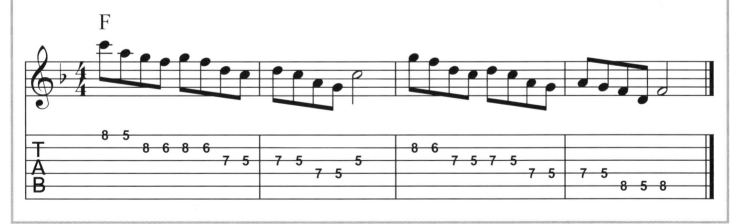

WEEK 36: F MINOR PENTATONIC

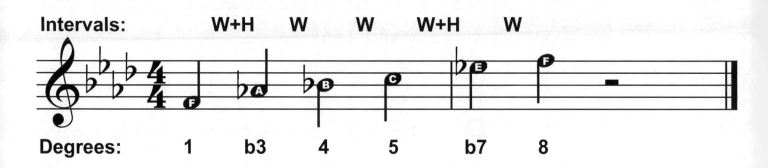

Intervals:		W+H	W	W	W+H	W
Degrees:	1	b3	4	5	b7	8

MONDAY: E SHAPE — 246

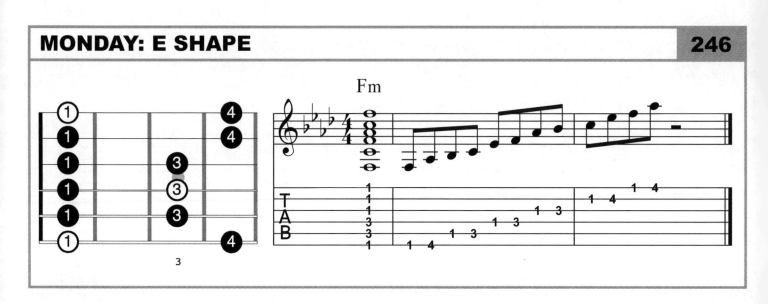

TUESDAY: D SHAPE — 247

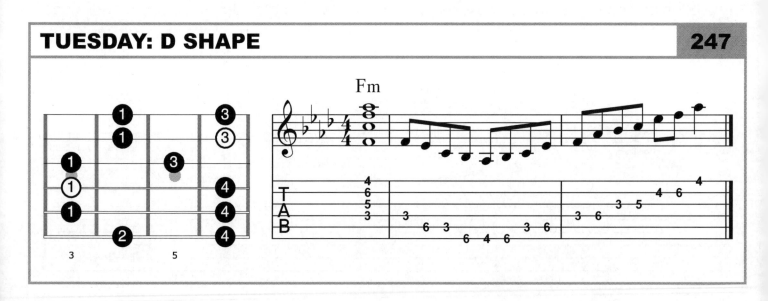

WEDNESDAY: C SHAPE

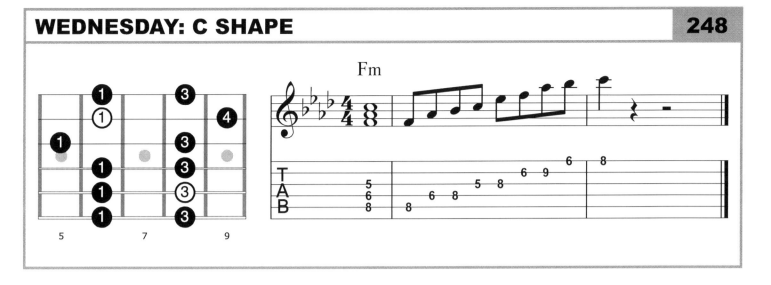

THURSDAY: A SHAPE

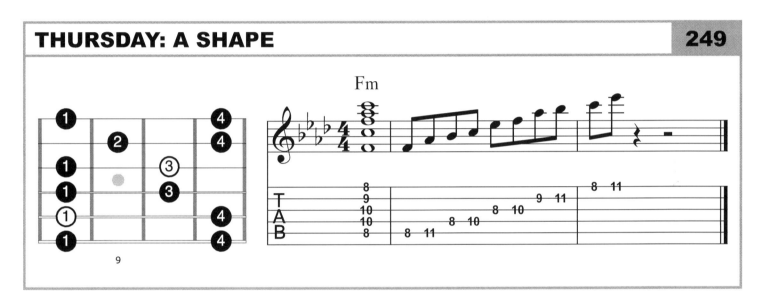

FRIDAY: G SHAPE

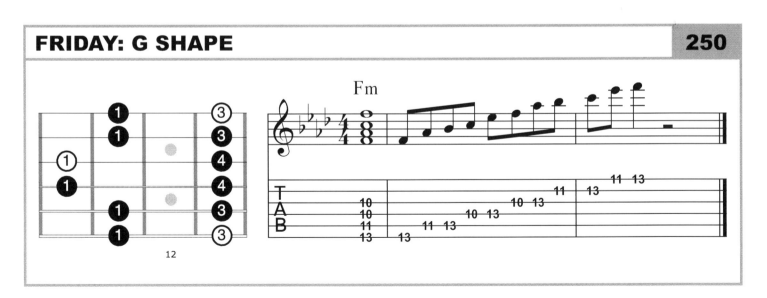

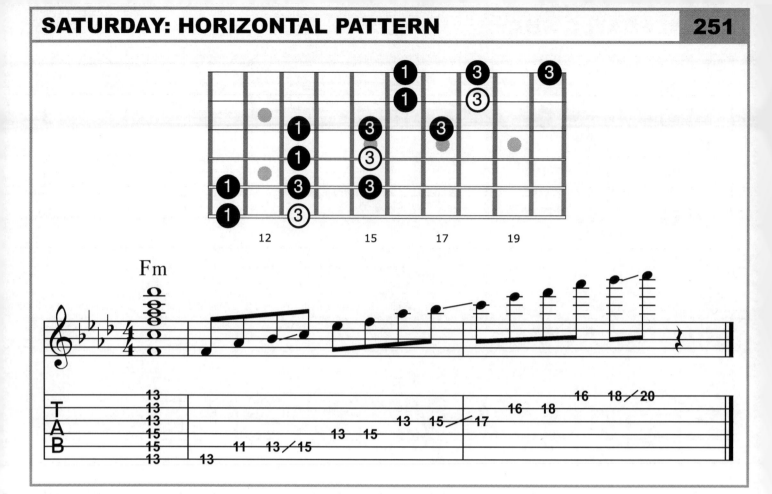

Ascending in 4s can also be accomplished by moving a pattern to a different set of strings. Try alternate picking every note or use a hammer-on to articulate each pair of notes.

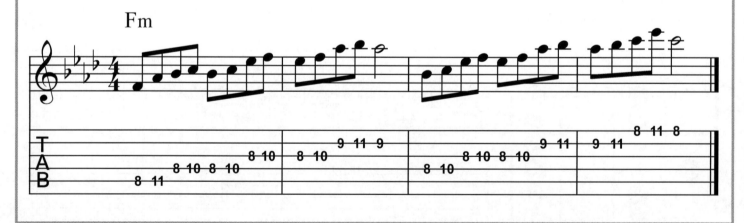

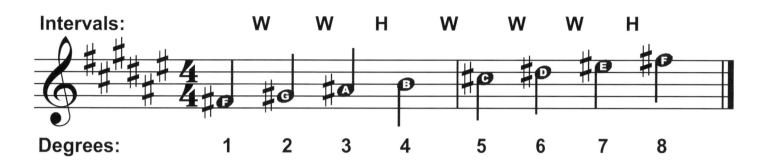

MONDAY: E SHAPE — 253

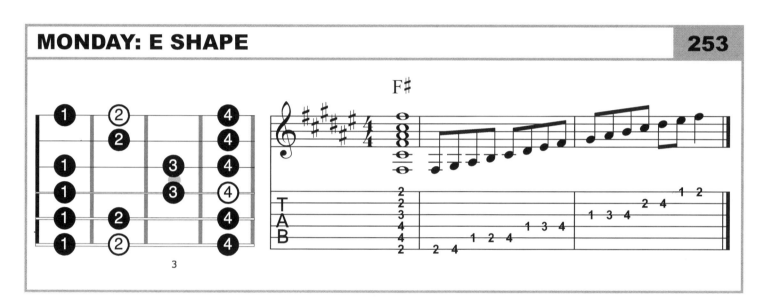

TUESDAY: D SHAPE — 254

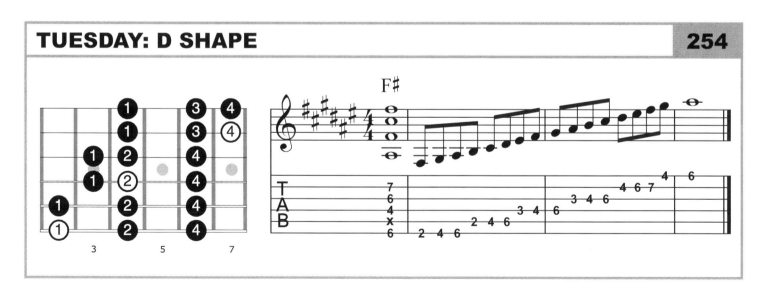

WEDNESDAY: C SHAPE

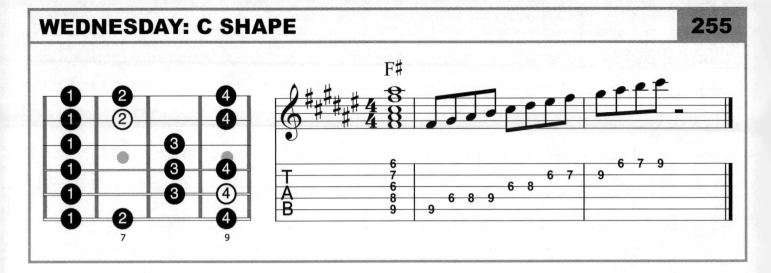

THURSDAY: A SHAPE

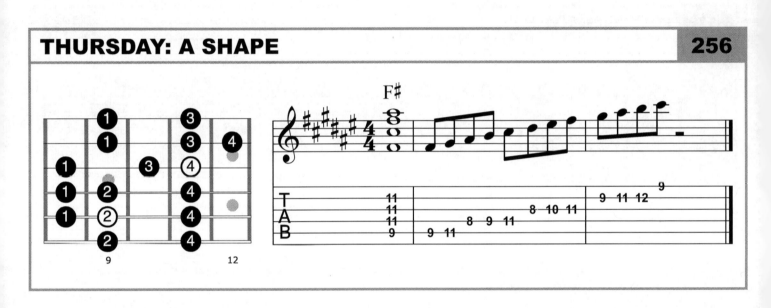

FRIDAY: G SHAPE

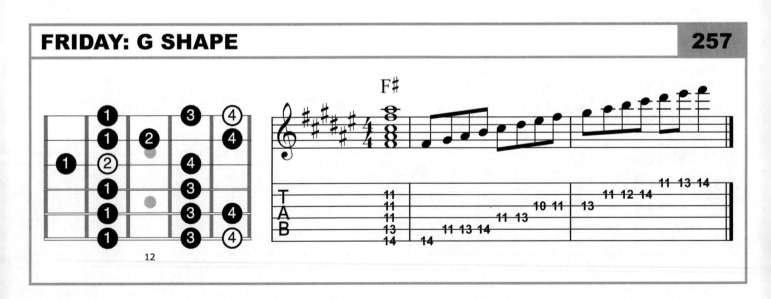

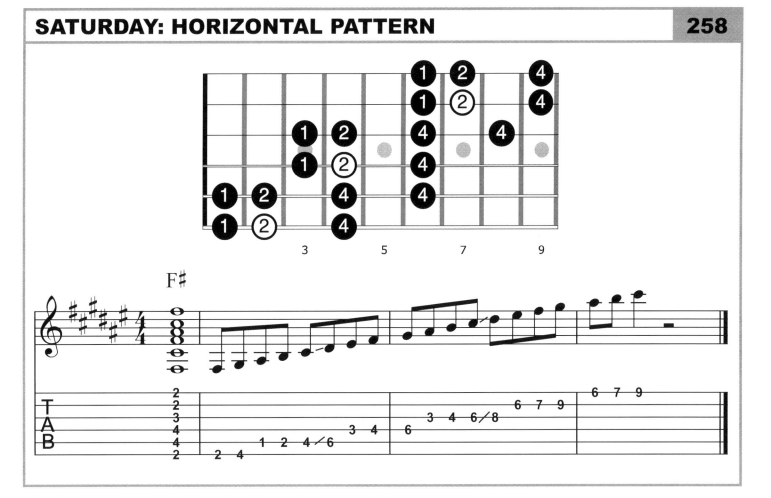

Horizontal patterns can be a great way to connect the CAGED patterns. This melody starts in the C Shape before shifting to the D Shape.

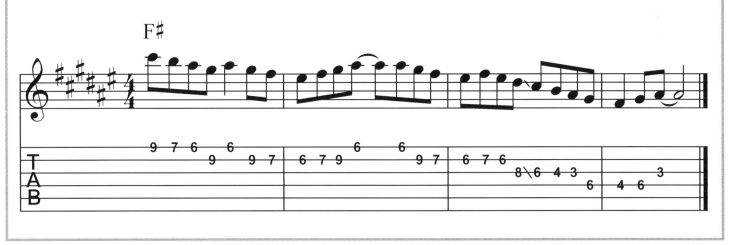

WEEK 38: F# MINOR

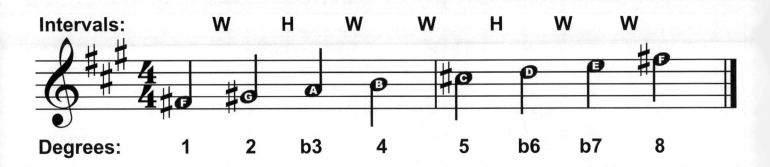

Intervals:	W	H	W	W	H	W	W

Degrees: 1   2   b3   4   5   b6   b7   8

MONDAY: E SHAPE   260

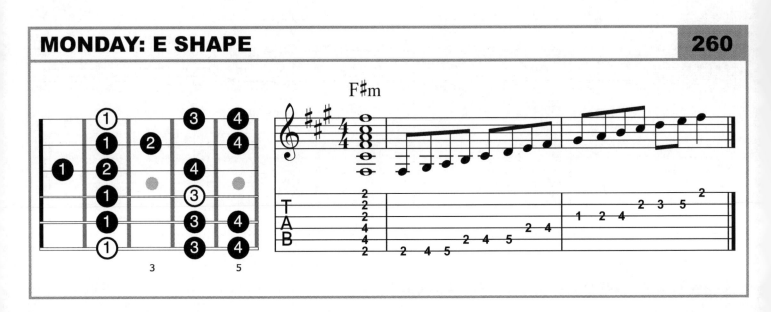

TUESDAY: D SHAPE   261

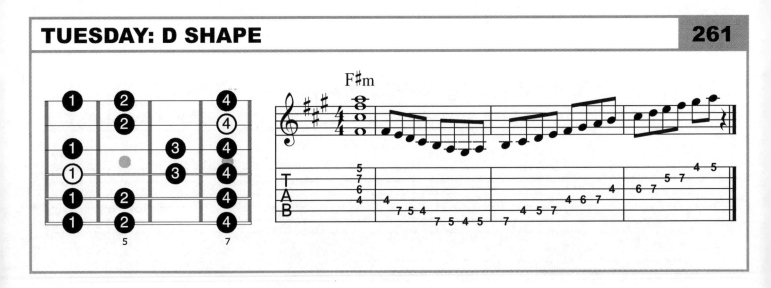

WEDNESDAY: C SHAPE

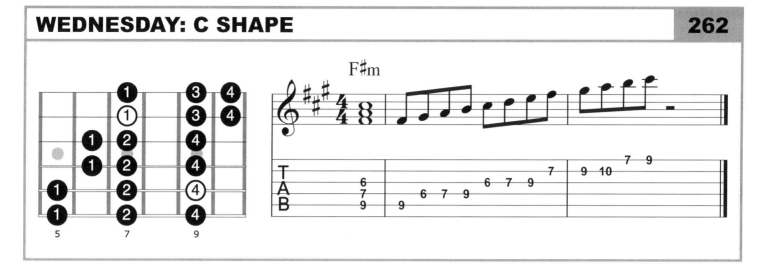

THURSDAY: A SHAPE

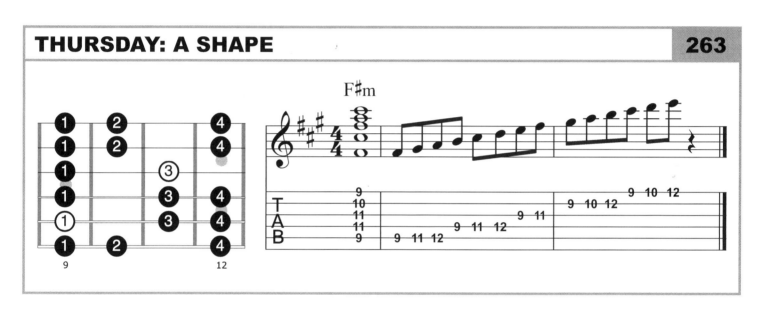

FRIDAY: G SHAPE

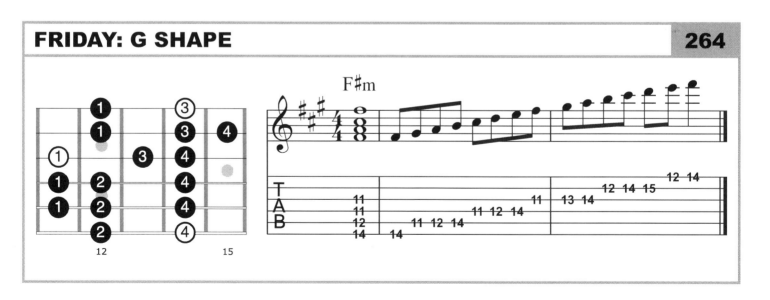

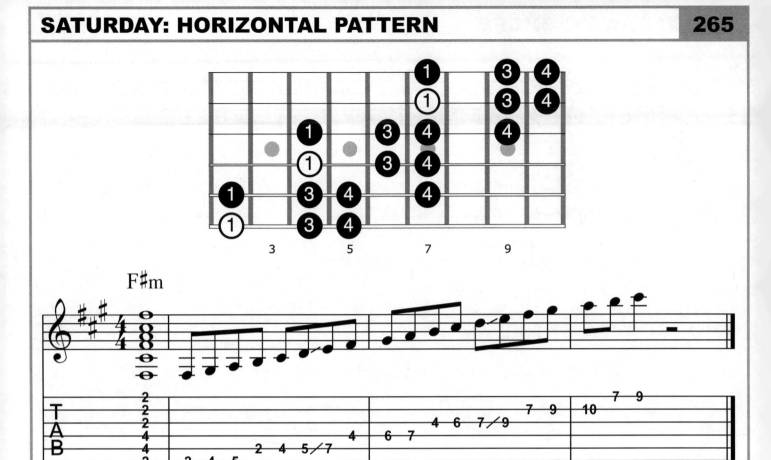

Many great riffs have been written in F♯ minor. This one uses the E Shape and will help prepare you for others using this position.

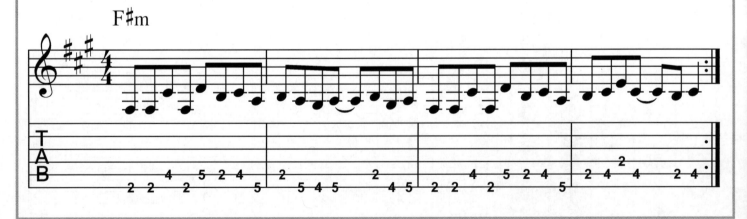

Intervals: W W W+H W W+H

Degrees: 1 2 3 5 6 8

MONDAY: E SHAPE | 267

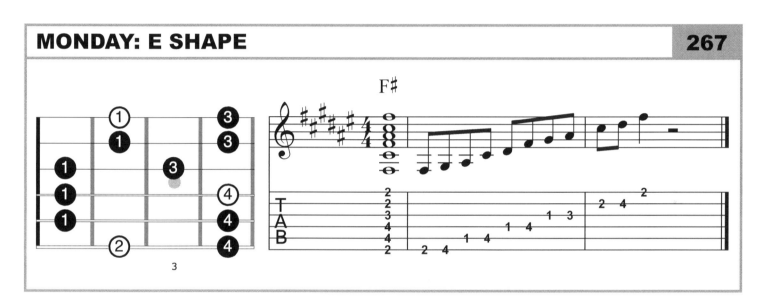

TUESDAY: D SHAPE | 268

WEDNESDAY: C SHAPE

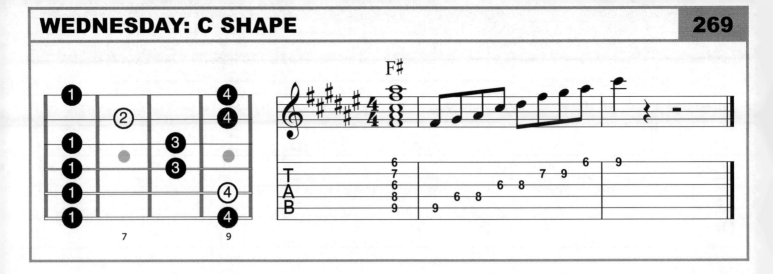

THURSDAY: A SHAPE

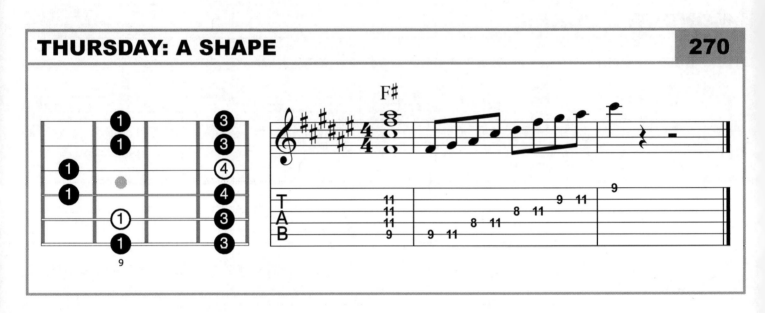

FRIDAY: G SHAPE

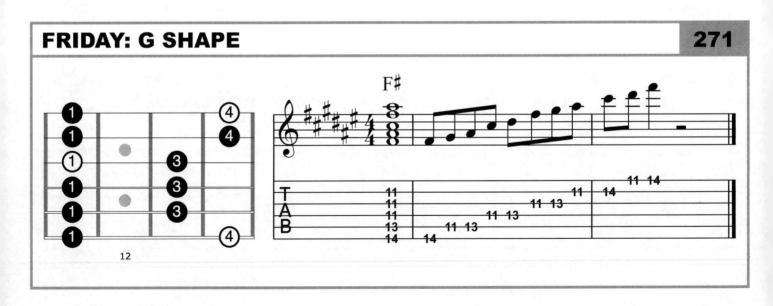

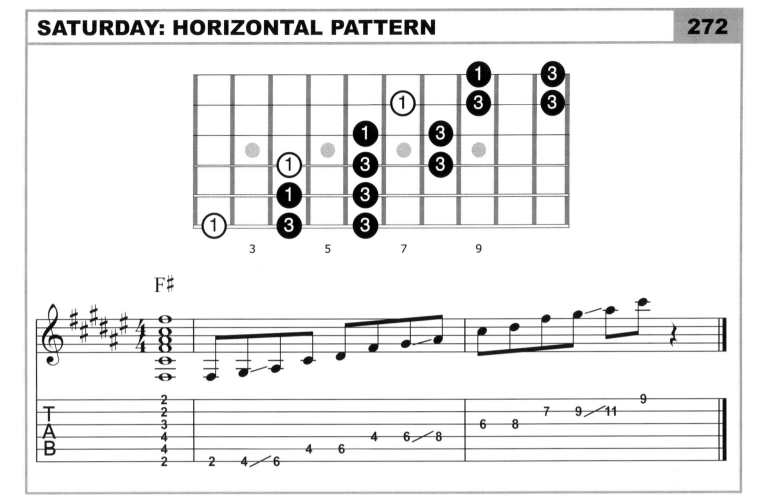

Another way you can break up stepwise scale motion is to change direction on every string. This provides a great opportunity to practice rolling your 1st and 3rd fingers. Fret the 2nd note with the pad of your first finger and then roll up to the tip as you cross strings. Continue this idea through the rest of the exercise.

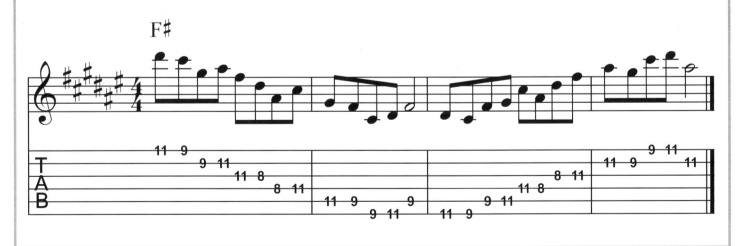

WEEK 40: F♯ MINOR PENTATONIC

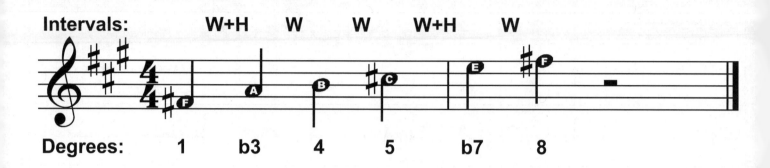

Intervals:		W+H	W	W	W+H	W
Degrees:	1	b3	4	5	b7	8

MONDAY: E SHAPE

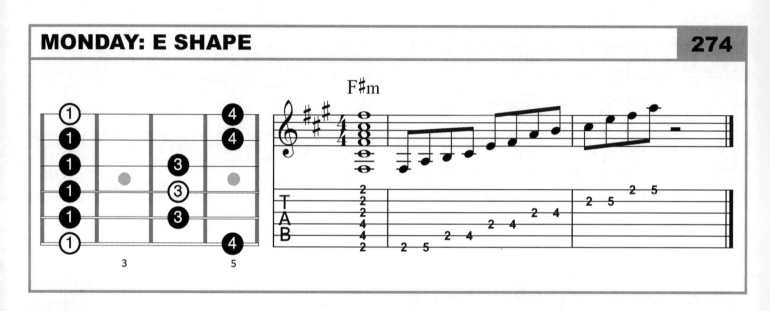

TUESDAY: D SHAPE

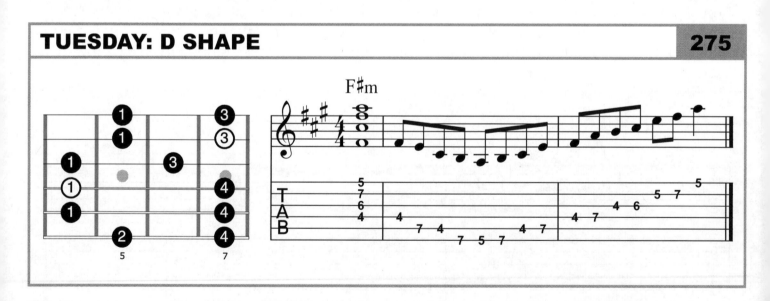

WEDNESDAY: C SHAPE

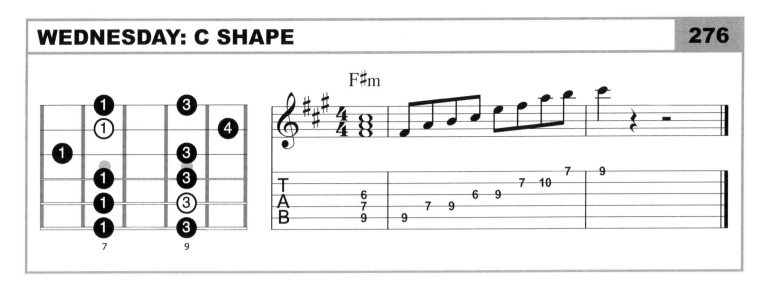

THURSDAY: A SHAPE

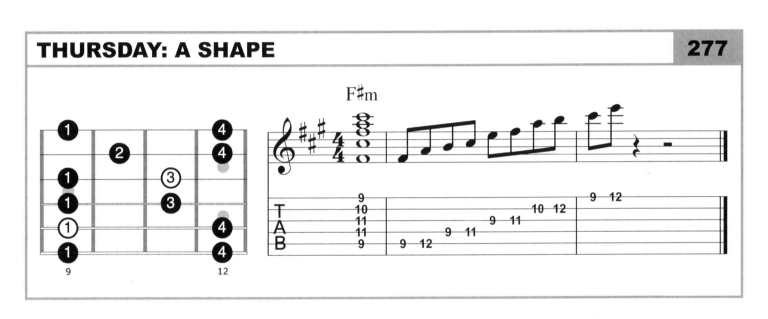

FRIDAY: G SHAPE

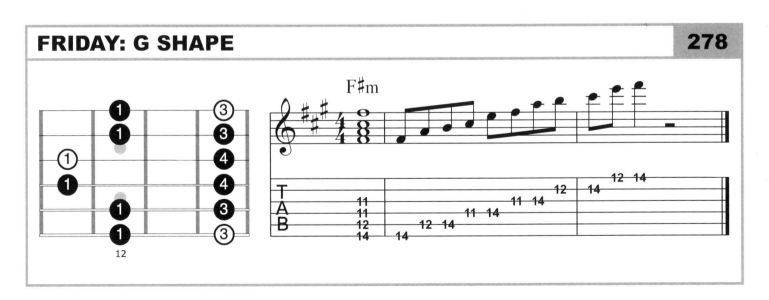

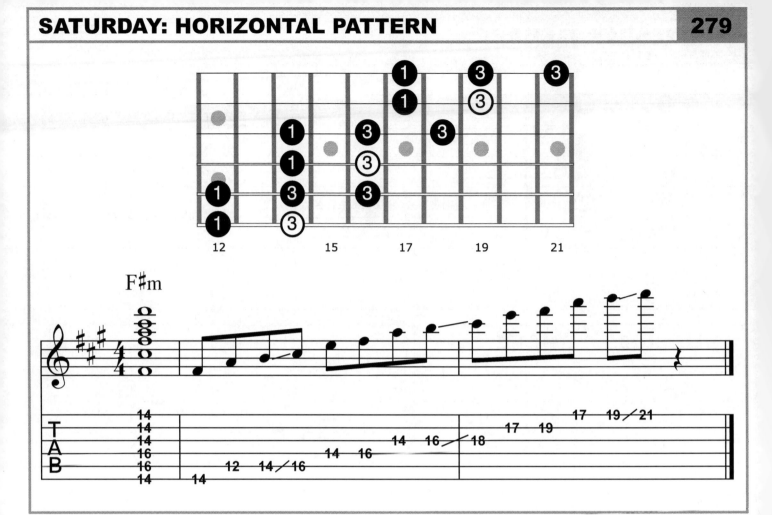

Changing direction can be effective in groups of 3. You can think of this pattern as 3 down/3 up. When played as 8th notes, this pattern creates a 3-against-4 rhythm that forces the pattern over the bar lines before returning to beat 1 in measure 4.

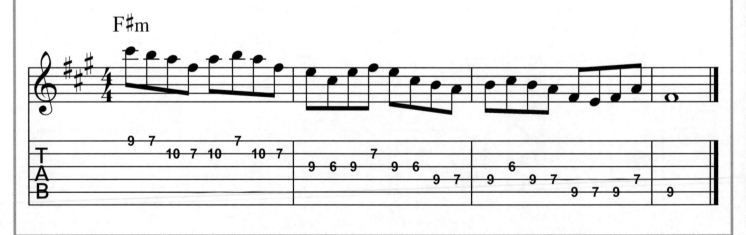

WEEK 41: G MAJOR

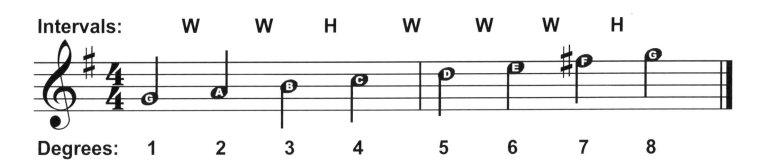

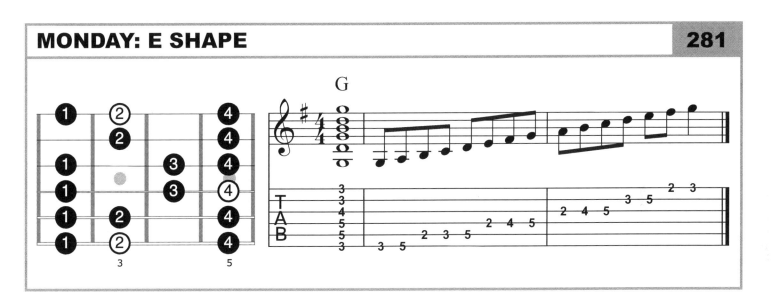

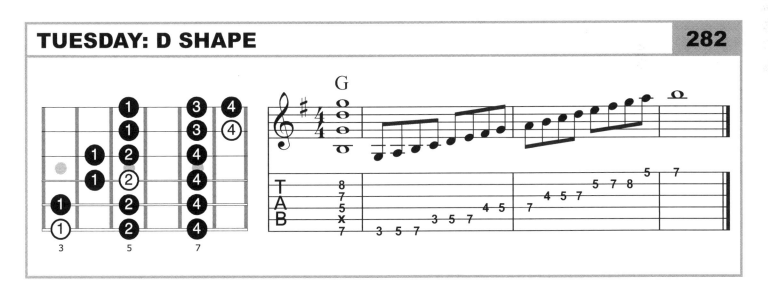

WEDNESDAY: C SHAPE

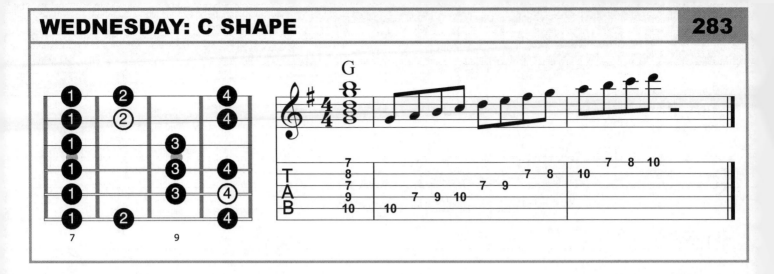

THURSDAY: A SHAPE

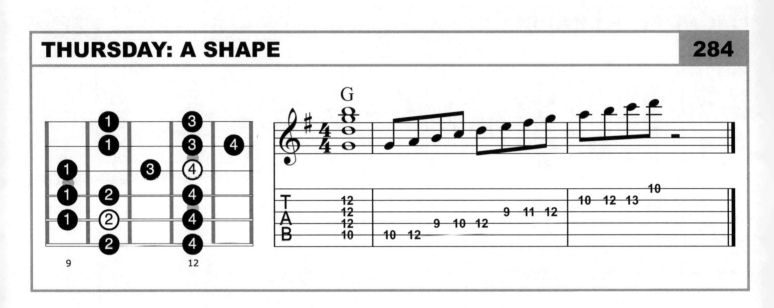

FRIDAY: G SHAPE

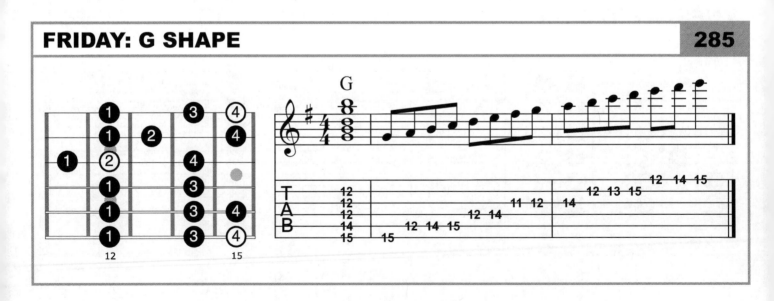

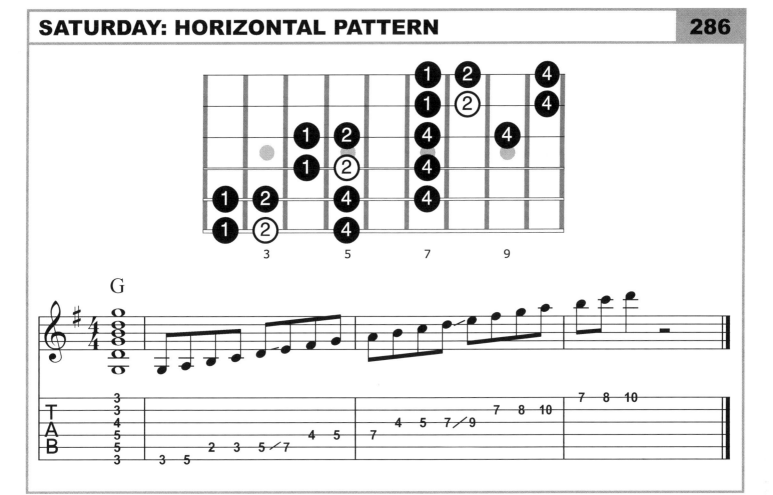

Horizontal patterns offer an opportunity to move a melodic idea through several octaves while maintaining the same fingering. To allow this with our next melody, our pattern's range is extended by two frets.

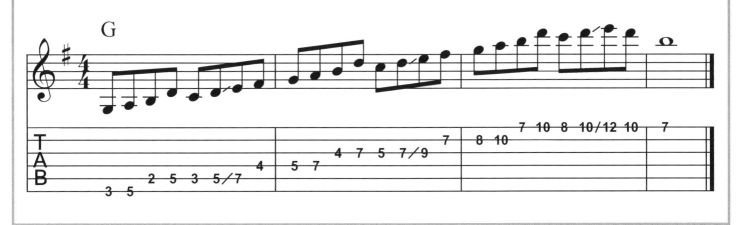

WEEK 42: G MINOR

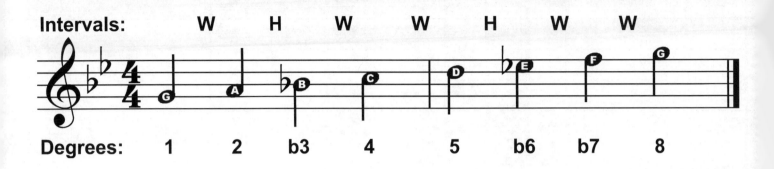

Intervals:		W		H		W		W		H		W		W	
Degrees:	1		2		b3		4		5		b6		b7		8

MONDAY: E SHAPE   288

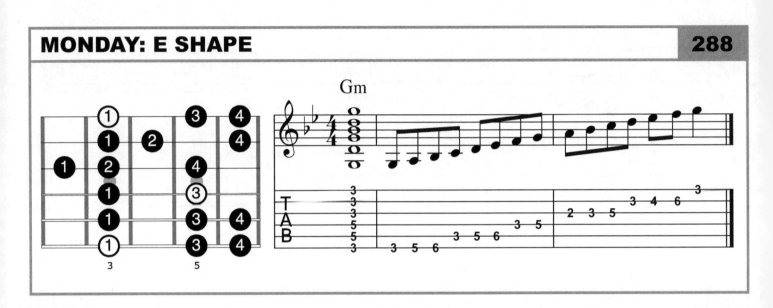

TUESDAY: D SHAPE   289

WEDNESDAY: C SHAPE

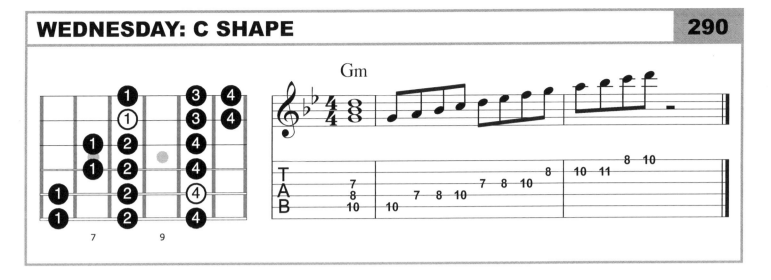

THURSDAY: A SHAPE

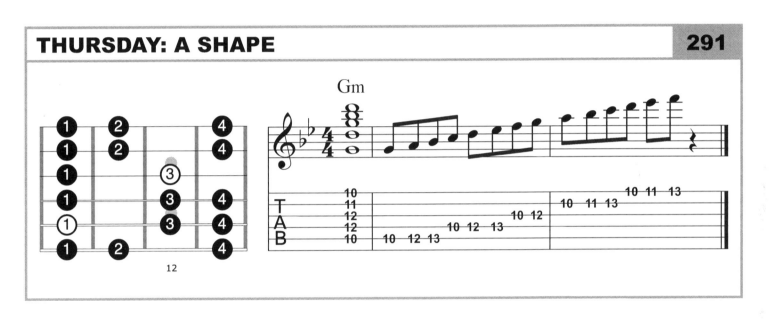

FRIDAY: G SHAPE

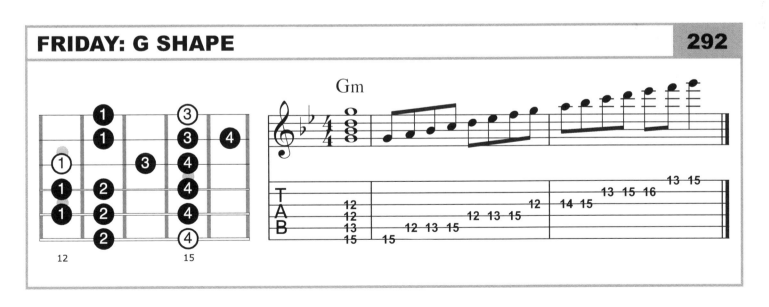

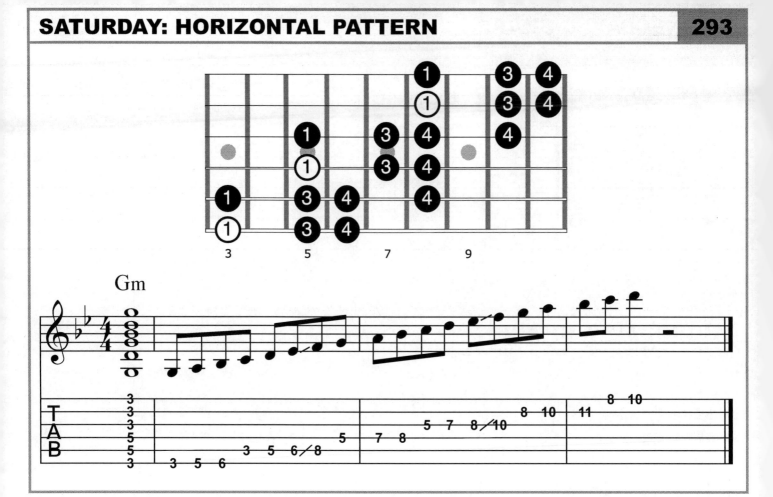

SUNDAY: SCALE APPLICATION   294

Now that you've learned some scale-pattern building blocks throughout this book, we'll begin to combine them into more dynamic phrases. While staying within the D Shape, this line uses ascending 4s, descending 3rds, and the down a 3rd/up 3 stepwise pattern before ending on the root.

WEEK 43: G MAJOR PENTATONIC

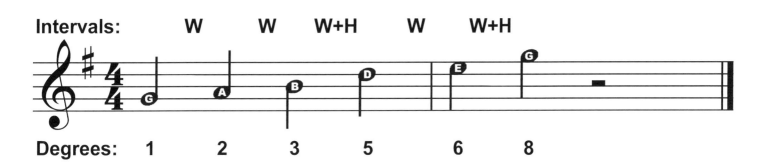

MONDAY: E SHAPE 295

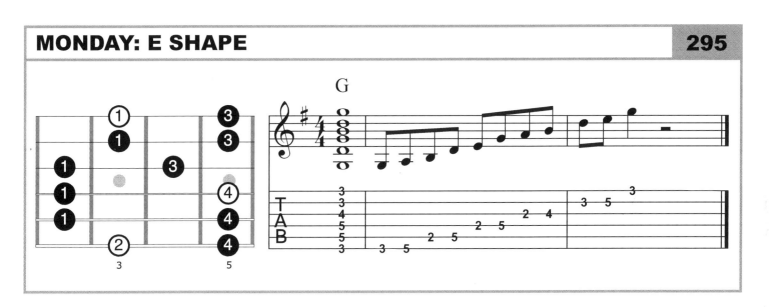

TUESDAY: D SHAPE 296

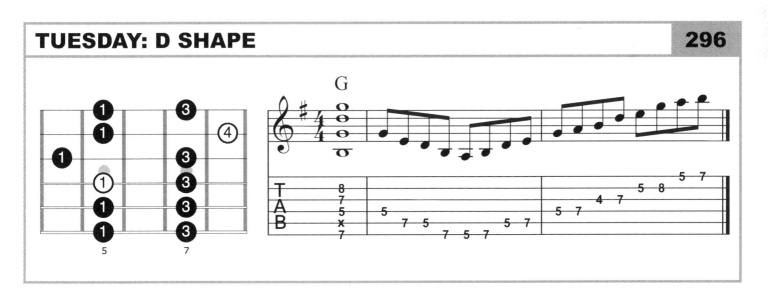

WEDNESDAY: C SHAPE

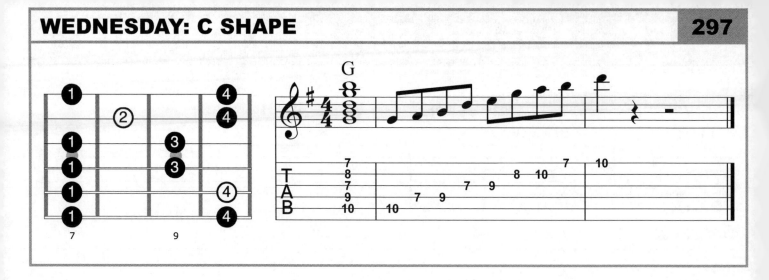

THURSDAY: A SHAPE

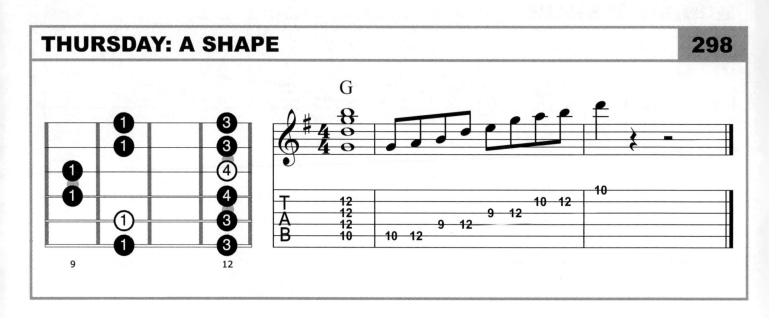

FRIDAY: G SHAPE

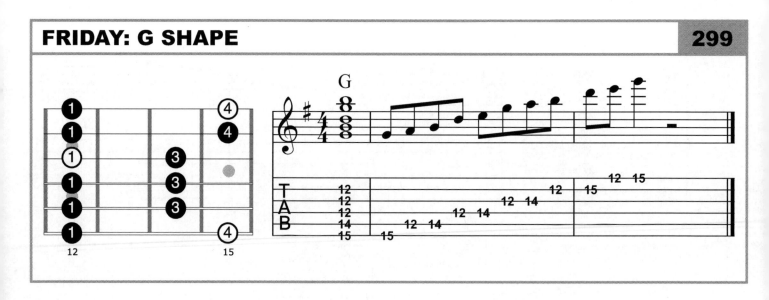

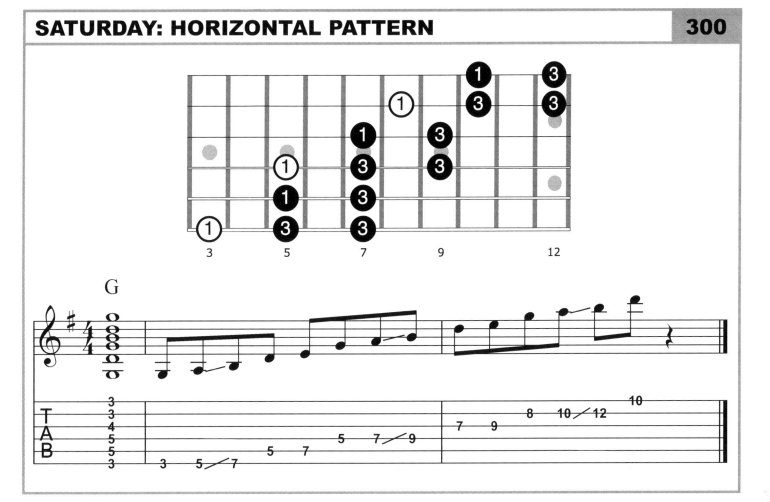

Changing direction in groups-of-3 patterns works equally well in ascending fashion. You could think of this pattern as up 3/down 3 as you move it across string pairs.

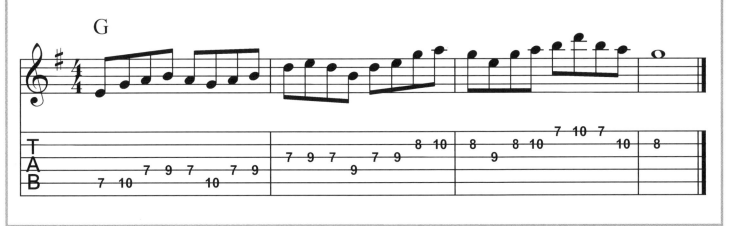

WEEK 44: G MINOR PENTATONIC

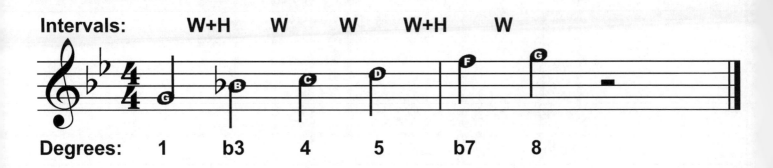

Intervals:	W+H	W	W	W+H	W

Degrees:	1	b3	4	5	b7	8

MONDAY: E SHAPE 302

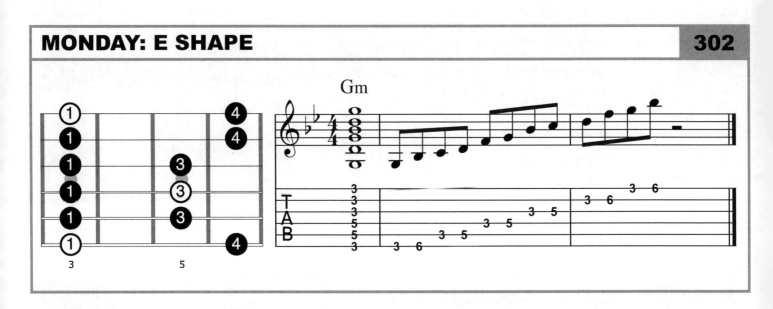

TUESDAY: D SHAPE 303

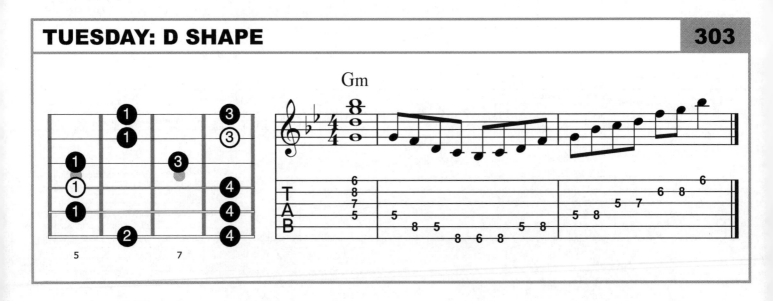

WEDNESDAY: C SHAPE

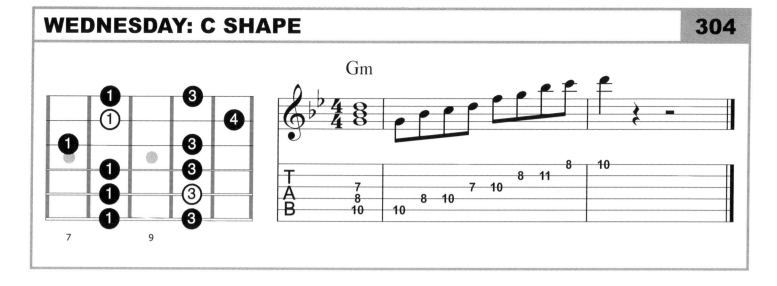

THURSDAY: A SHAPE

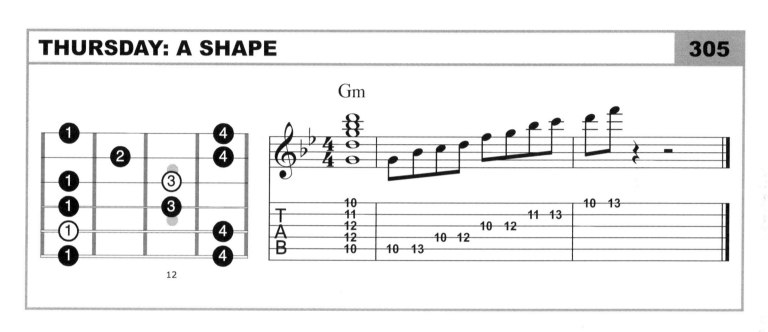

FRIDAY: G SHAPE

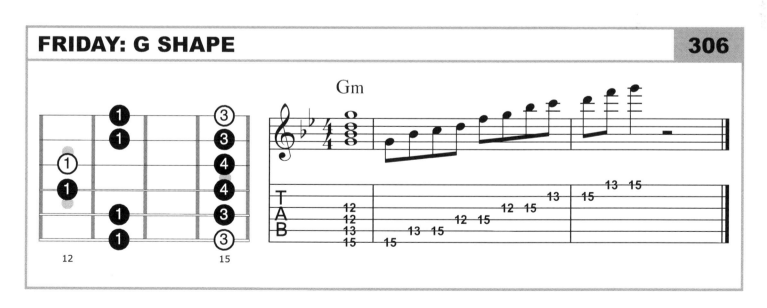

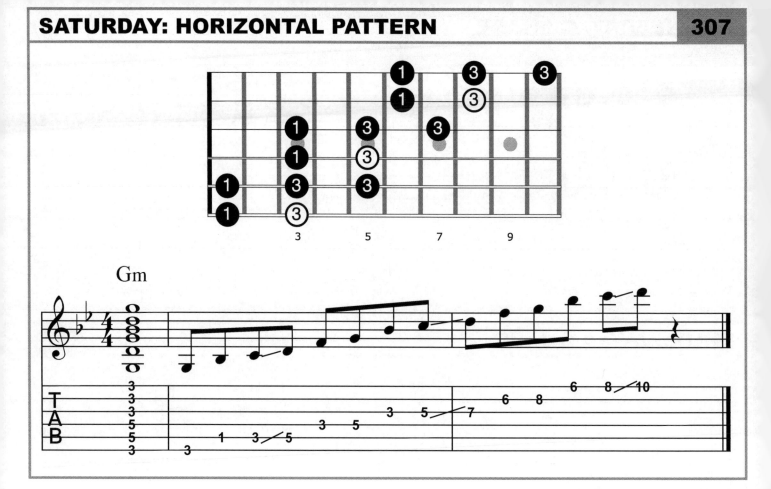

SUNDAY: SCALE APPLICATION

Changing direction in groups of 3 fits like a glove when using triplets, and triplets fit like a glove when playing blues. This phrase uses the upper range of the Horizontal Pattern, an area used frequently by guitarists. As an option, you can perform the 3rd-string slides with your 2nd finger.

WEEK 45: A♭ MAJOR

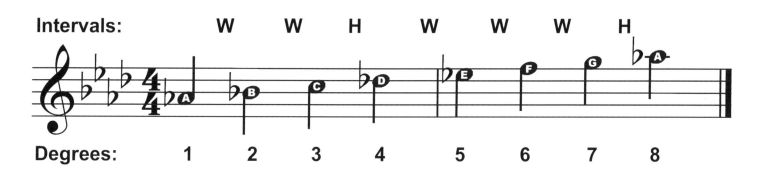

Intervals: W   W   H   W   W   W   H

Degrees: 1   2   3   4   5   6   7   8

MONDAY: E SHAPE   309

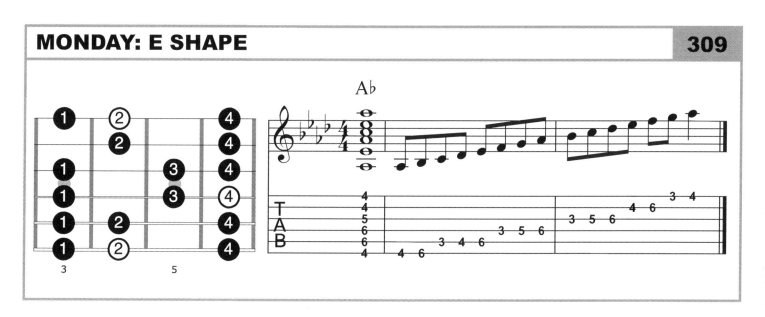

TUESDAY: D SHAPE   310

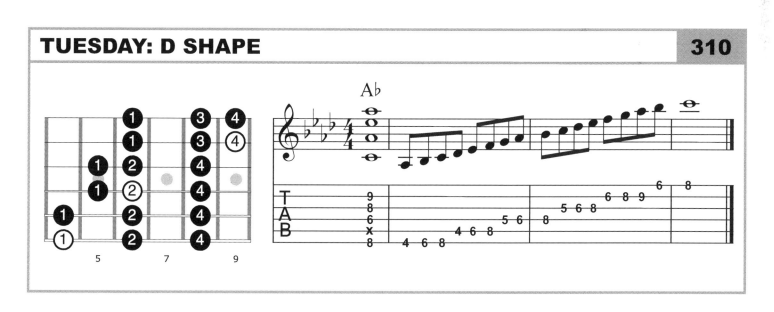

WEDNESDAY: C SHAPE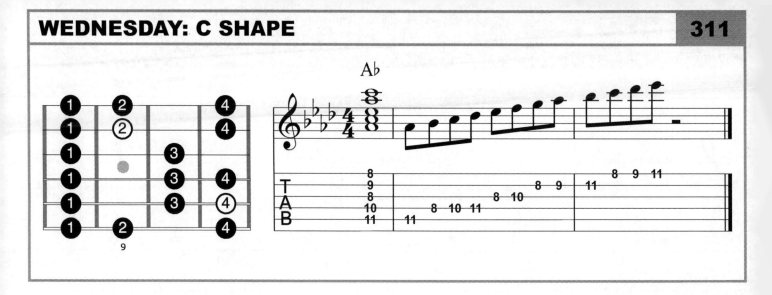

311

THURSDAY: A SHAPE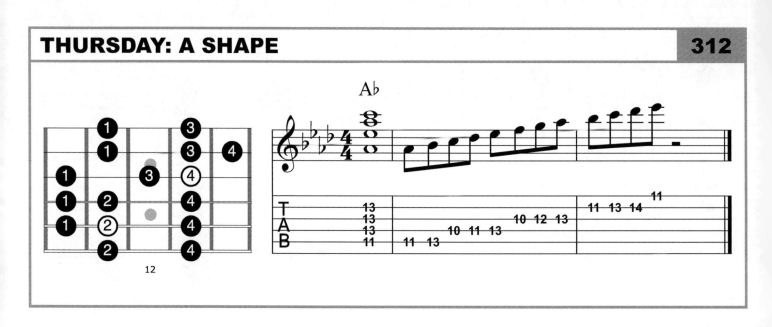

312

FRIDAY: G SHAPE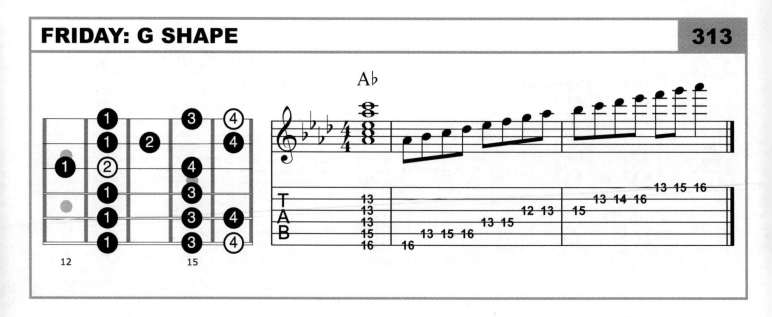

313

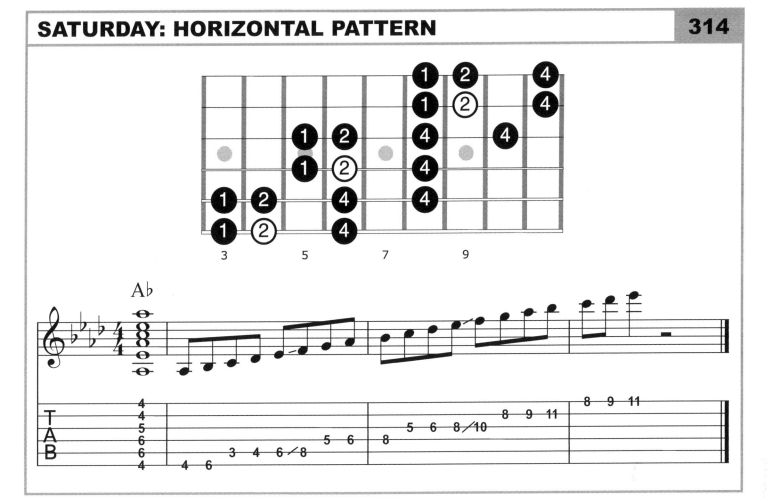

This phrase mixes up the vocabulary you've learned so far. It starts in the D Shape with a descending 3rd/up 3 stepwise pattern, then uses the Horizontal Pattern to get to the C Shape, where you'll encounter ascending 3s. These lead us to an ascending 3rd/down 3 stepwise pattern, descending 3rds, and a horizontal shift back to the D Shape.

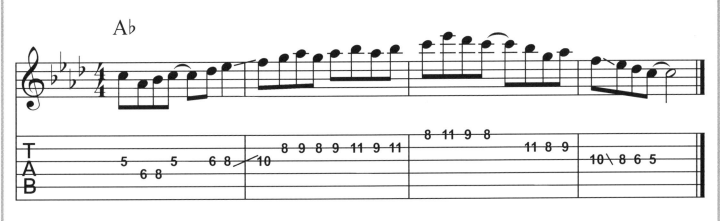

WEEK 46: A♭ MINOR

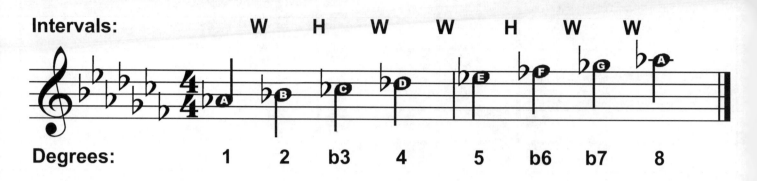

Intervals:		W	H	W	W	H	W	W
Degrees:		1	2	b3	4	5	b6	b7	8

MONDAY: G SHAPE 316

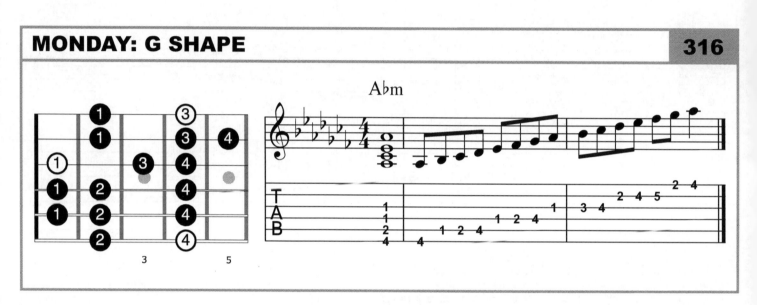

TUESDAY: E SHAPE 317

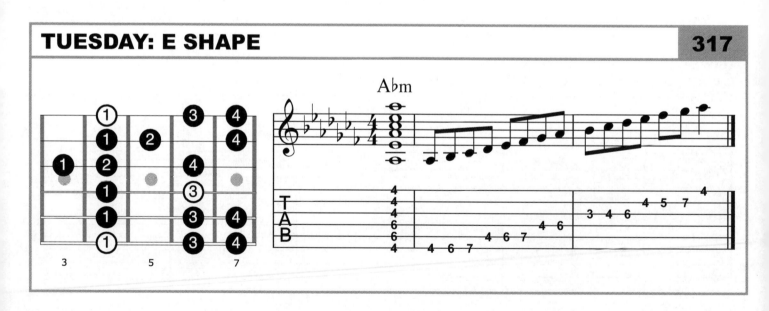

144

WEDNESDAY: D SHAPE

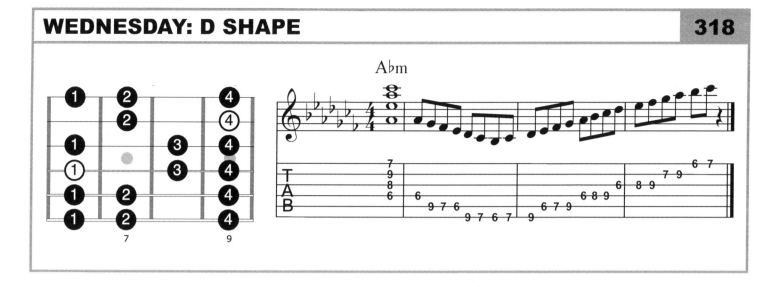

THURSDAY: C SHAPE

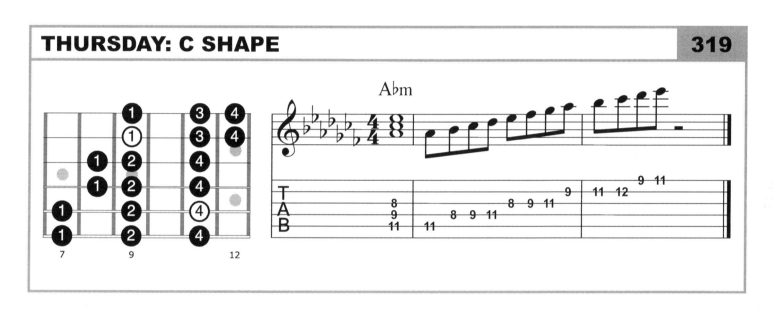

FRIDAY: A SHAPE

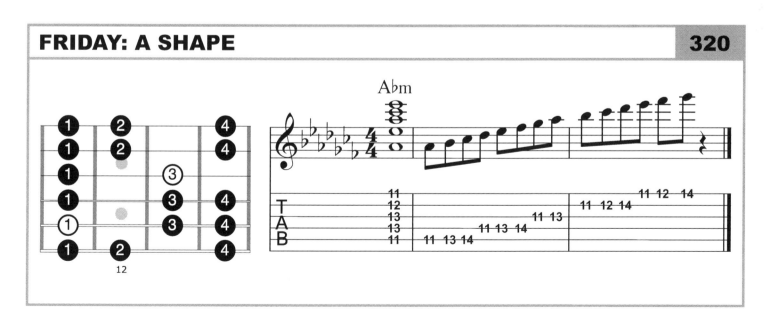

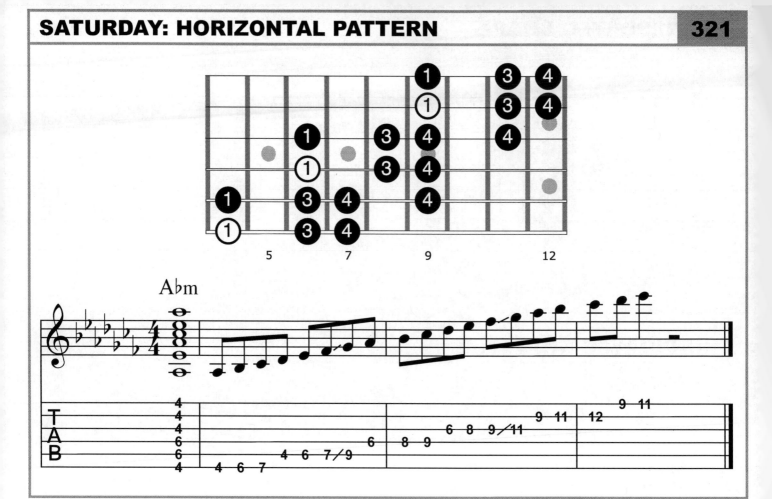

SUNDAY: SCALE APPLICATION 322

In this, our final minor scale example, we'll continue to explore melodic devices that shift between the minor pentatonic and full minor scale. Sometimes melodies require changing a scale fingering. In measure 3, shift with your 1st finger.

WEEK 47: A♭ MAJOR PENTATONIC

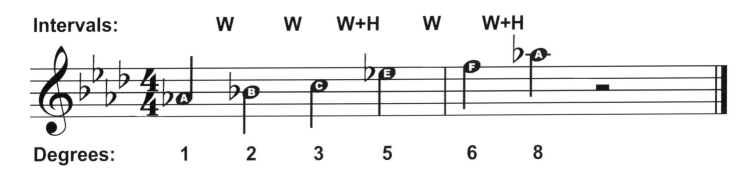

Intervals: W   W   W+H   W   W+H

Degrees: 1   2   3   5   6   8

MONDAY: G SHAPE   323

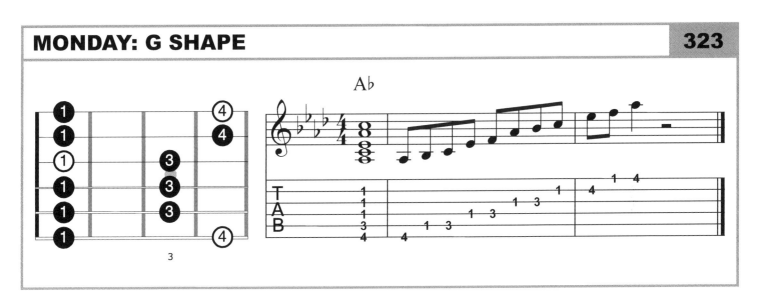

TUESDAY: E SHAPE   324

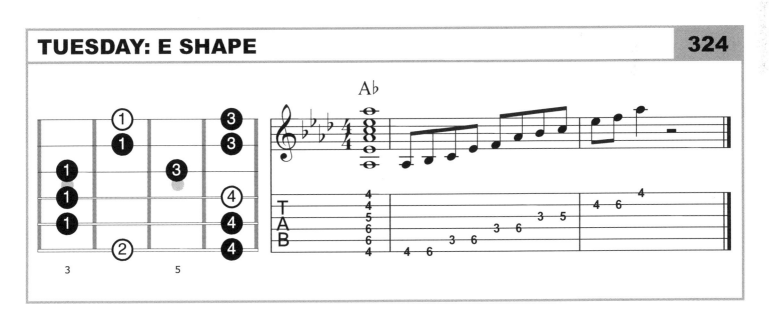

147

WEDNESDAY: D SHAPE

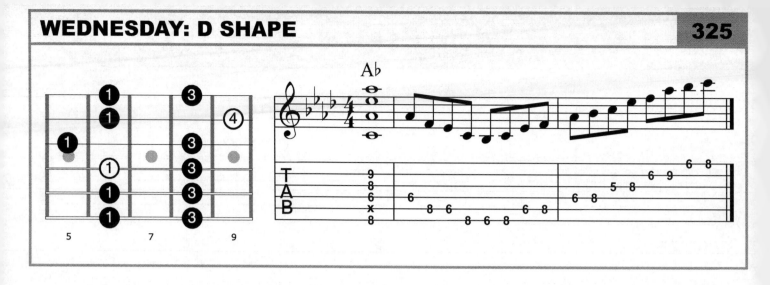

THURSDAY: C SHAPE

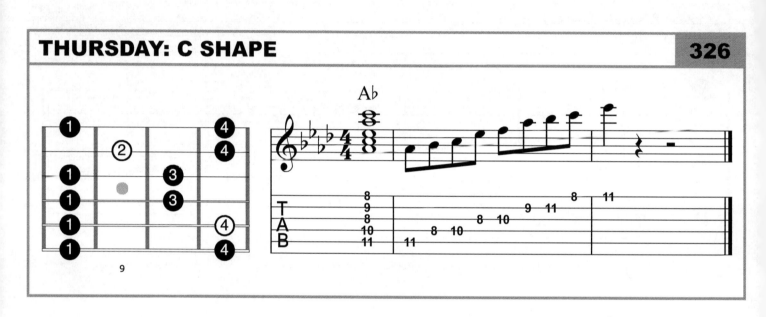

FRIDAY: A SHAPE

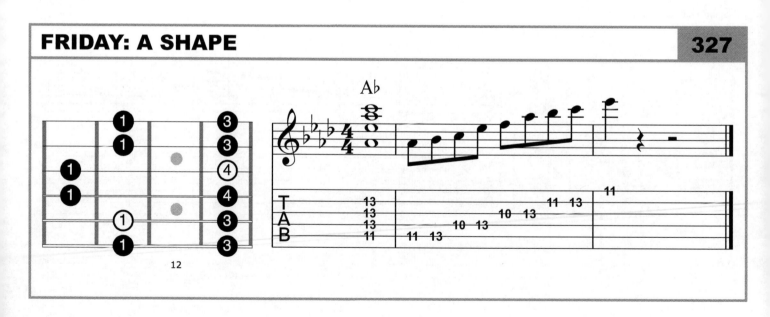

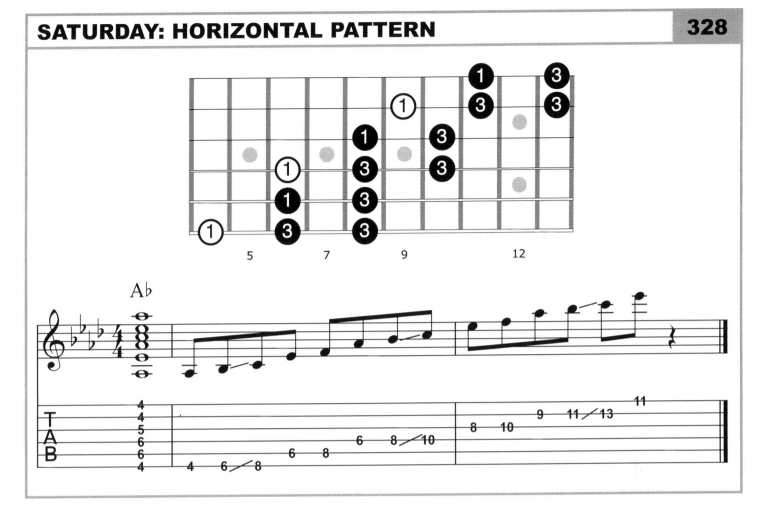

For our final pentatonic scale sequences, we'll explore groups of 6. Notice how it descends the D Shape until the last three notes, where it utilizes the Horizontal Pattern to end on the root.

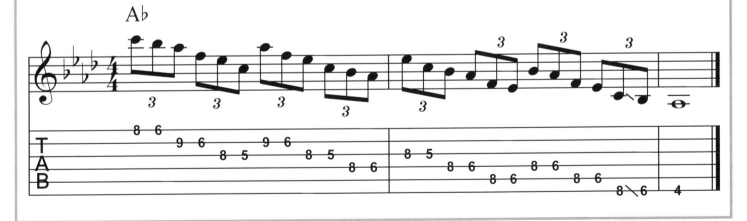

WEEK 48: A♭ MINOR PENTATONIC

Intervals: W+H   W   W   W+H   W

Degrees: 1   b3   4   5   b7   8

MONDAY: G SHAPE | 330

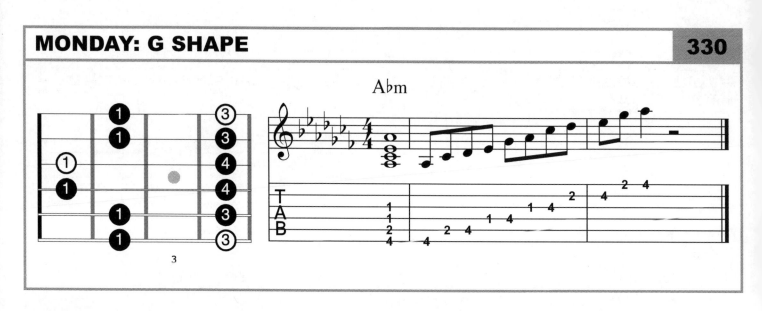

A♭m

TUESDAY: E SHAPE | 331

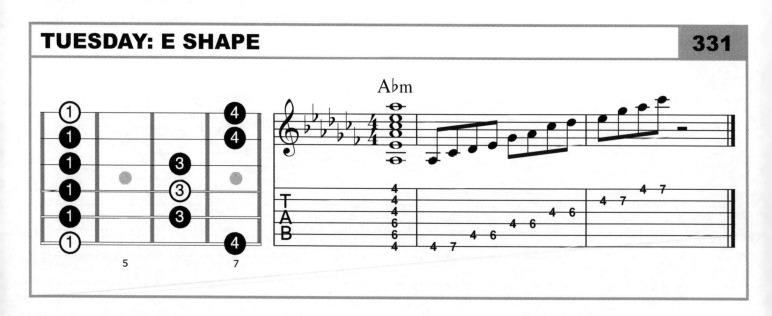

A♭m

WEDNESDAY: D SHAPE

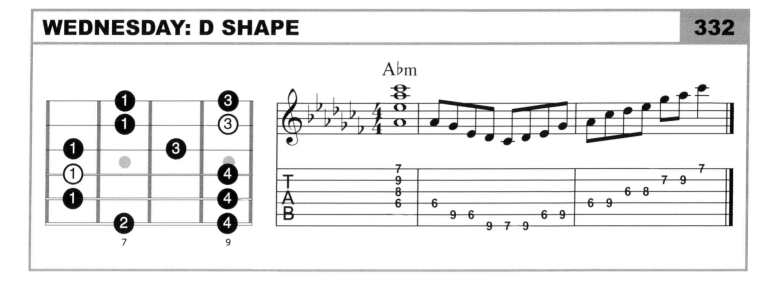

THURSDAY: C SHAPE

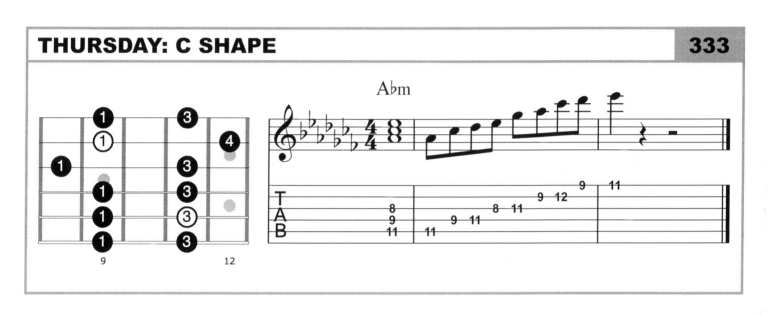

FRIDAY: A SHAPE

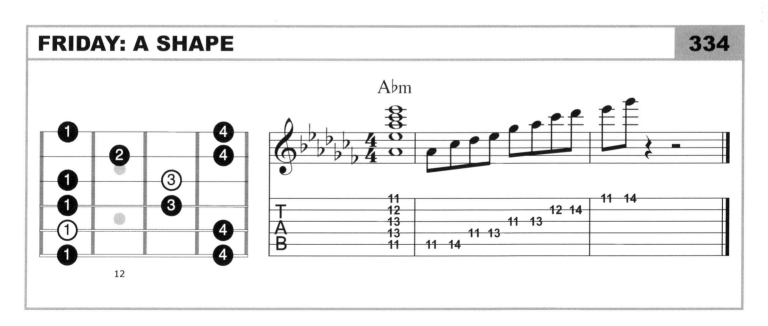

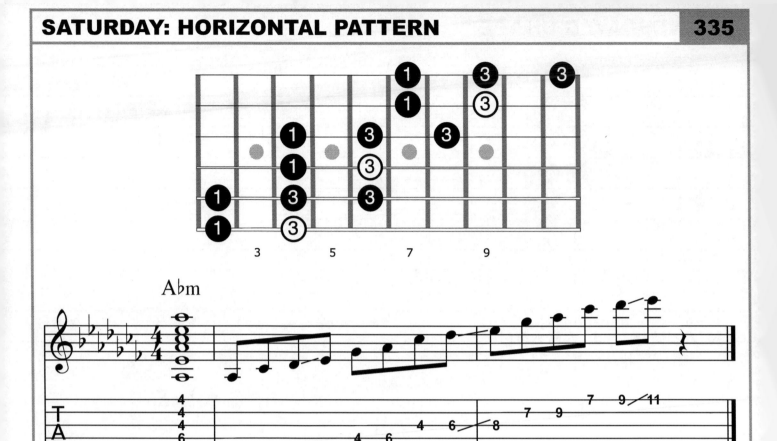

Our final pentatonic sequence changes direction from last week, ascending the E Shape in groups of 6. Use alternate picking or a picked note followed by a hammer-on.

WEEK 49: THE BLUES SCALE

The *blues scale* is a very popular modification of the minor pentatonic scale that you already know and is used in many styles of music. The ♭5th, commonly referred to as the "blue note," is added to the minor pentatonic formula.

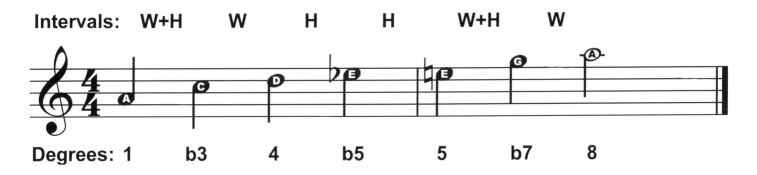

Intervals:	W+H	W	H	H	W+H	W
Degrees: 1	b3	4	b5	5	b7	8

MONDAY: G SHAPE 337

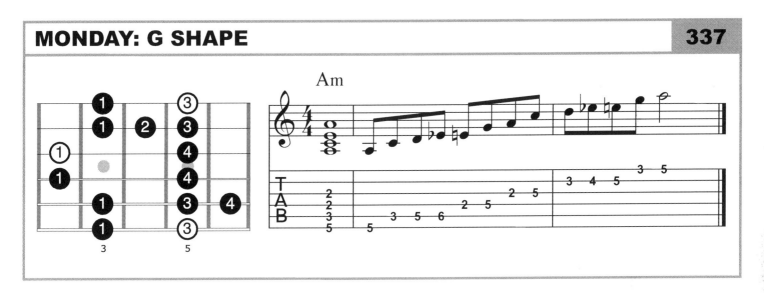

TUESDAY: E SHAPE 338

WEDNESDAY: D SHAPE

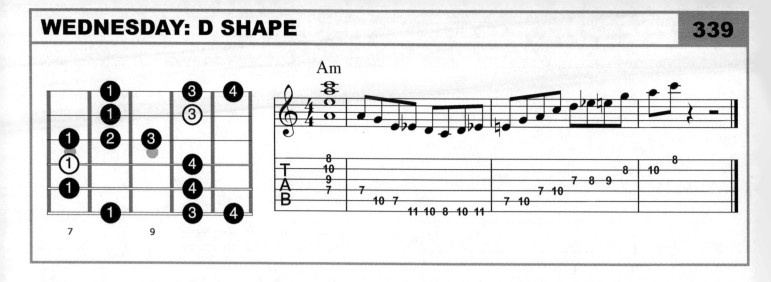

THURSDAY: C SHAPE

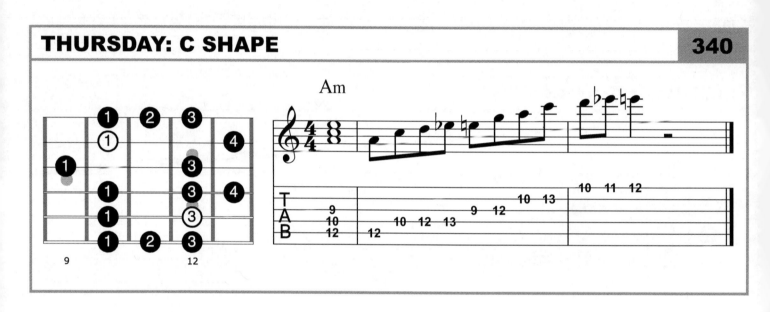

FRIDAY: A SHAPE

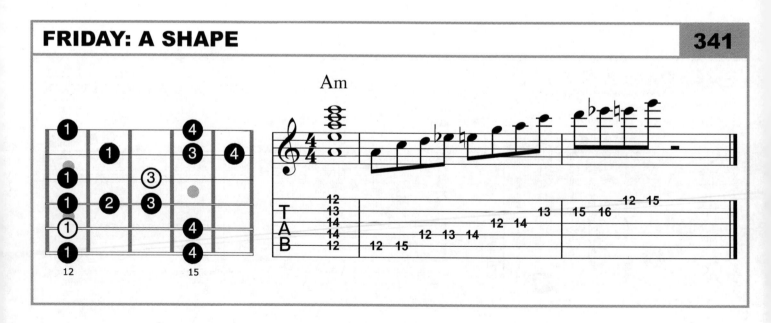

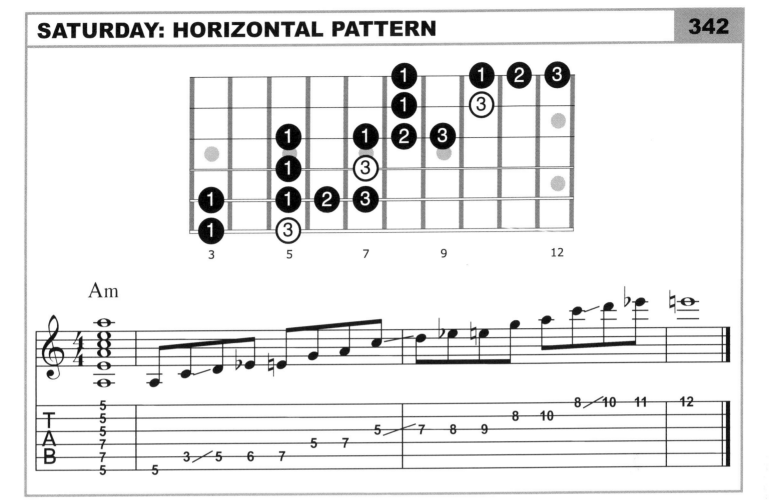

SUNDAY: SCALE APPLICATION

343

Can I combine different scale patterns at will? Of course! One of the great attributes of horizontal patterns is that you can use them to get to a new place on the fretboard, as in our example below.

WEEK 50: HARMONIC MINOR

The *harmonic minor scale* is a popular modification of the natural minor scale. The 7th degree of the harmonic minor scale is raised to a major 7th, creating increased pull back towards the root note.

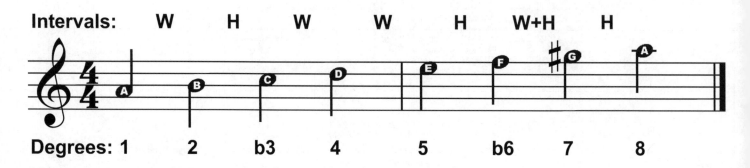

MONDAY: G SHAPE   344

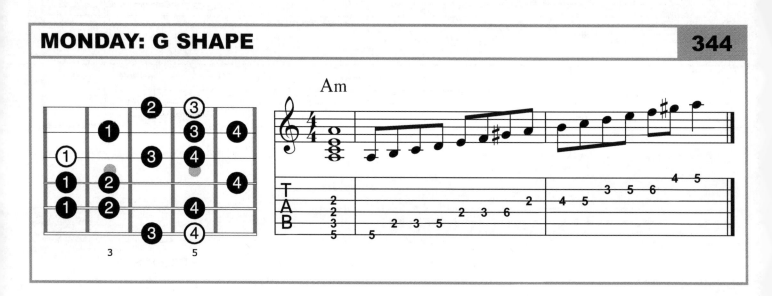

TUESDAY: E SHAPE   345

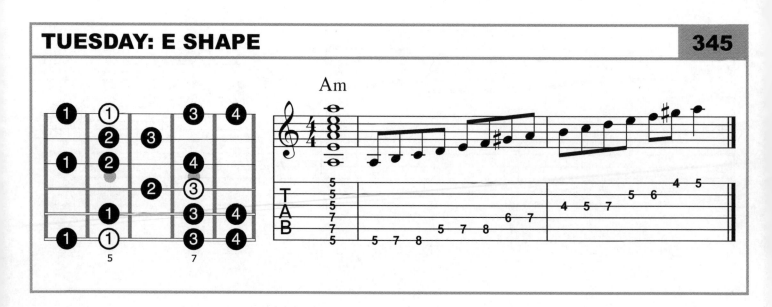

WEDNESDAY: D SHAPE

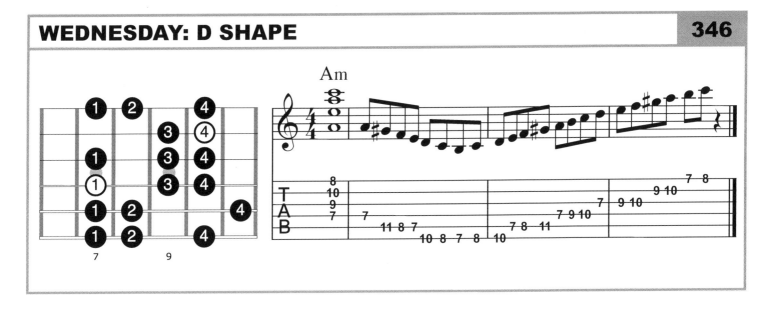

THURSDAY: C SHAPE

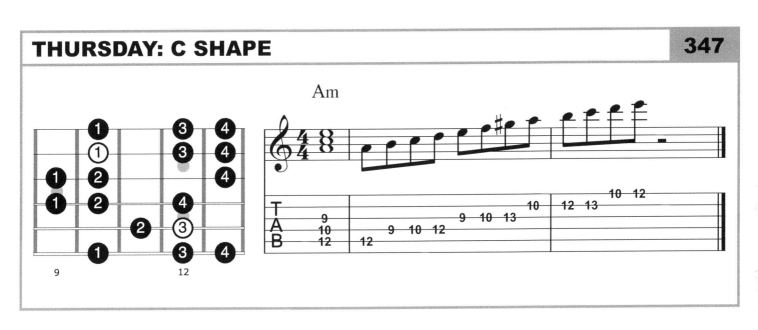

FRIDAY: A SHAPE

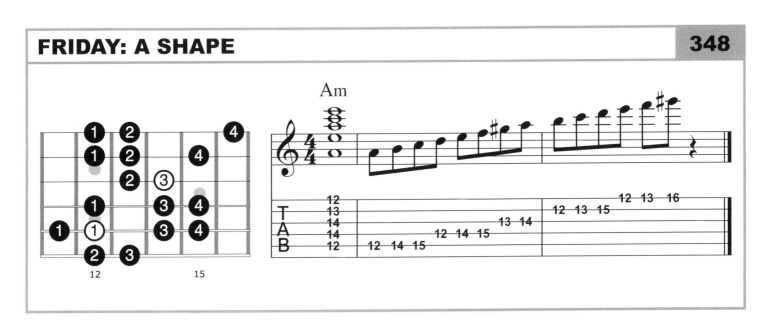

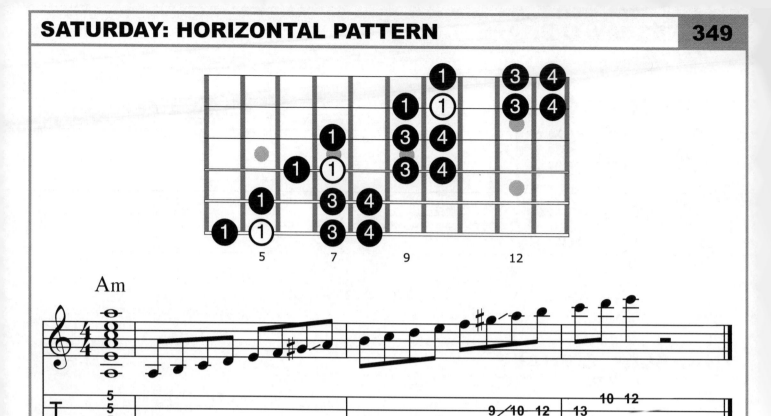

The harmonic minor scale is heavily used in classical music. The following example is written in that style. How many musical devices that you've previously learned can you spot?

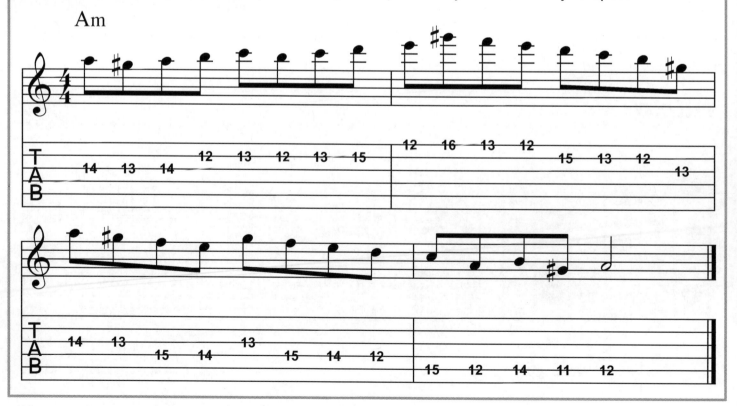

WEEK 51: MELODIC MINOR

The *melodic minor scale* utilizes a major 6th and major 7th scale degree. You can think of it as raising the 6th and 7th of the natural minor scale, or lowering the 3rd of the major scale. "Yesterday" by the Beatles is a great example of its sound and usage.

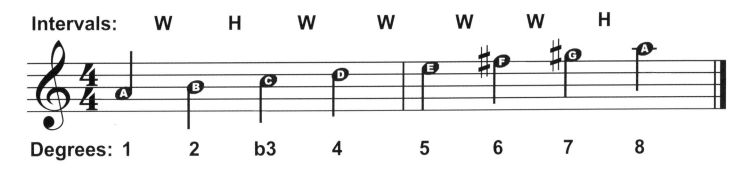

Intervals:	W	H	W	W	W	W	H
Degrees: 1	2	b3	4	5	6	7	8

MONDAY: G SHAPE 351

TUESDAY: E SHAPE 352

WEDNESDAY: D SHAPE

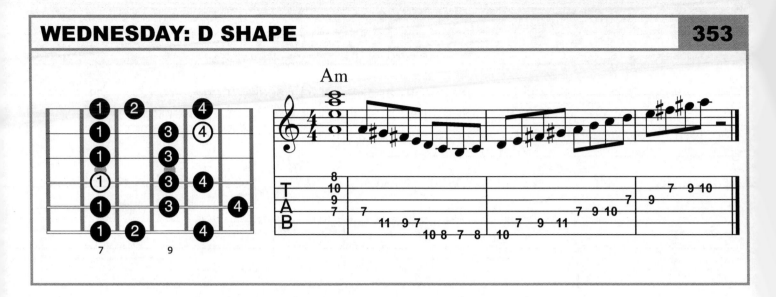

THURSDAY: C SHAPE

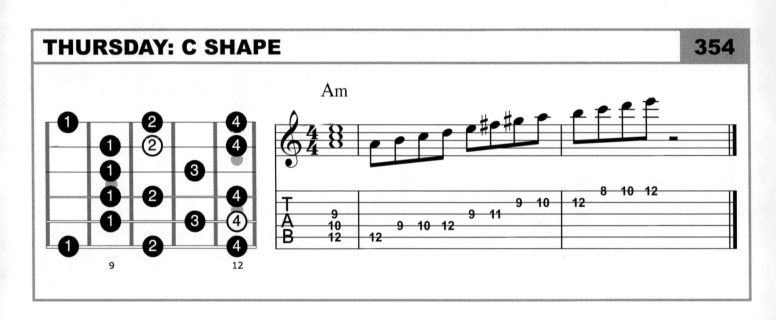

FRIDAY: A SHAPE

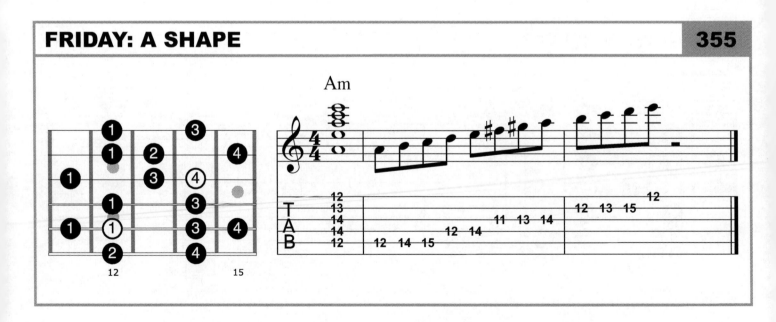

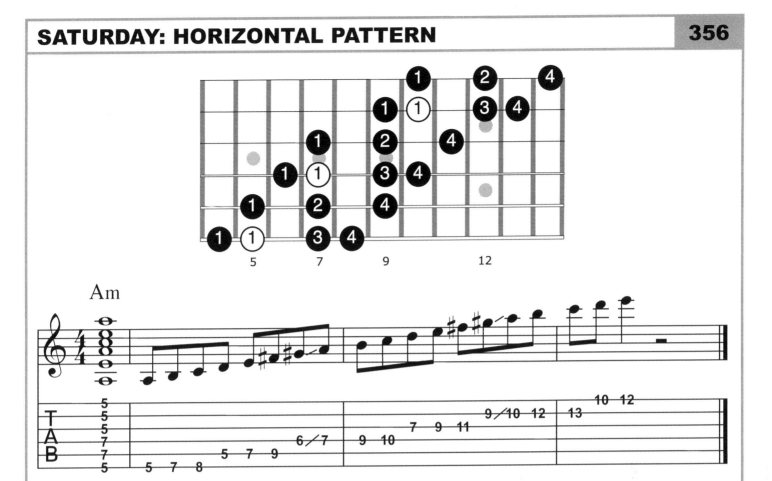

Melodic minor is often used in jazz, the style of our phrase below. Notice the use of 3rd intervals. Each group of four 8th notes could be thought of as a melodic cell (the first cell is used twice).

WEEK 52: THE MODES

Throughout this book, we've been examining how the starting note of a scale directly influences its sound. By changing the starting pitch of the major scale, we create a new interval pattern as the scale returns to that starting pitch eight notes higher. Since there are seven notes in the major scale, there are seven different scale degrees to start from, and these new scales are commonly referred to as "The Modes." The modes have been in use since the Middle Ages and are based on Greek music theory. They are named after different regions of Greece and are still referred to by their Greek names.

Each mode has its own sound, or musical flavor. Let's explore how this works by using the key of G major and its C-Shape pattern. Let's start by reviewing the construction of the G major scale.

IONIAN: THE MAJOR SCALE

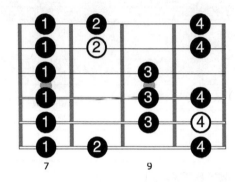

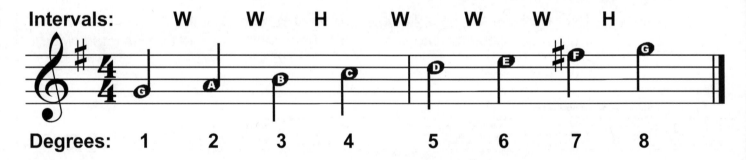

Intervals: W   W   H   W   W   W   H

Degrees: 1   2   3   4   5   6   7   8

To build the Dorian mode, we simply start on the 2nd note of the G major scale, playing the scale from A to A. By doing so, we have made the A note the 1st scale degree, or root, and we now call the scale "A Dorian."

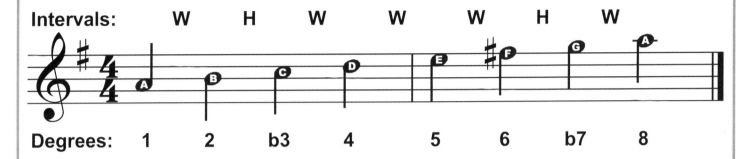

Intervals:	W	H	W	W	W	H	W

Degrees:	1	2	b3	4	5	6	b7	8

Notice how the interval pattern has shifted? In analyzing what is different from the standard A major scale, you'll find the 3rd and 7th degrees have been lowered. When you have a lowered 3rd, the scale is considered minor.

On the fretboard, we'll shift the C Shape's starting note (and chord) by one note, as well. Observe the positioning of the white dots.

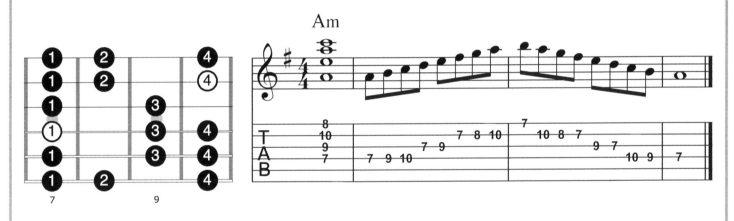

To build the B Phrygian mode, start the G major scale from its 3rd note, playing the scale from B to B. When compared to B major, you'll find a lowered 2nd, 3rd, 6th, and 7th. The presence of a lowered 3rd makes it a minor scale.

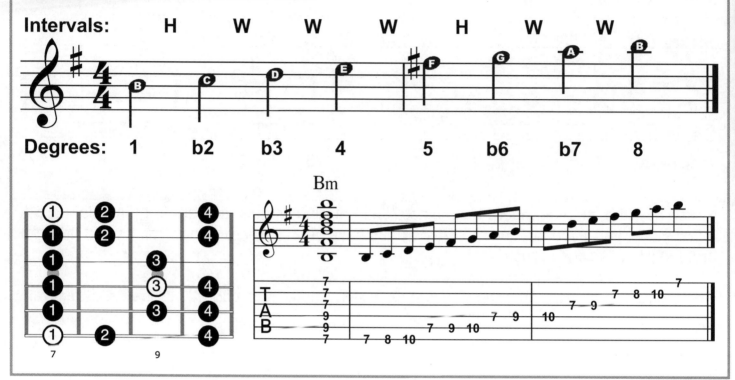

To build C Lydian, we'll start the G major scale from its 4th note. Doing so raises the 4th scale degree of the standard C major scale and provides us with a new major sound.

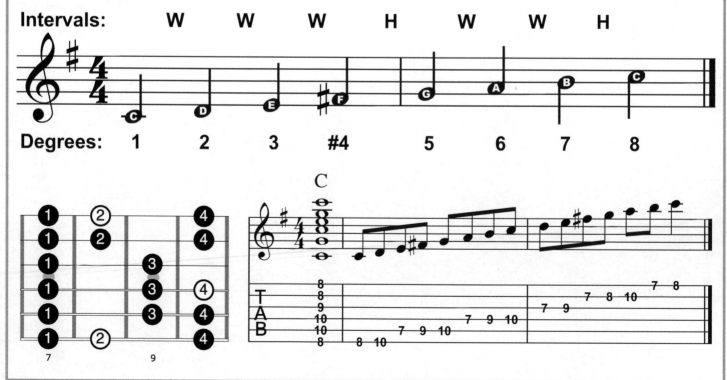

D Mixolydian is created by playing G major from its 5th step. You could think of it as a major scale with a lowered 7th.

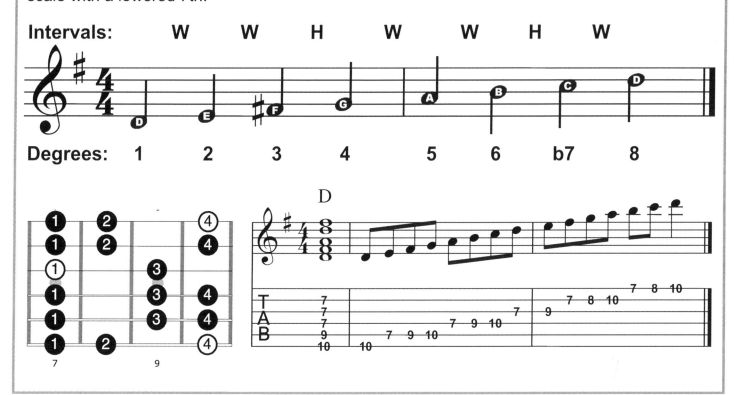

Intervals:	W	W	H	W	W	H	W
Degrees:	1	2	3	4	5	6	b7	8

Playing G major from its 6th degree creates E Aeolian. It's the most used mode and we've been playing it throughout the book, as it's also referred to as the natural minor scale.

Intervals:	W	H	W	W	H	W	W
Degrees:	1	2	b3	4	5	b6	b7	8

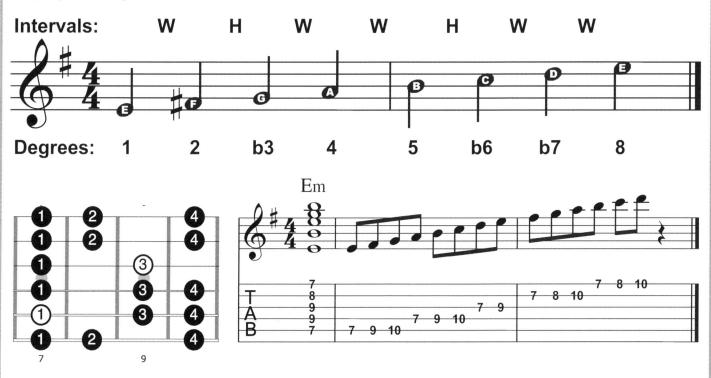

SATURDAY: LOCRIAN

Our last mode, F♯ Locrian, is built by playing G major from its 7th degree. Of all the modes, Locrian contains the most alterations. Playing the root, lowered 3rd, and lowered 5th together creates a diminished chord.

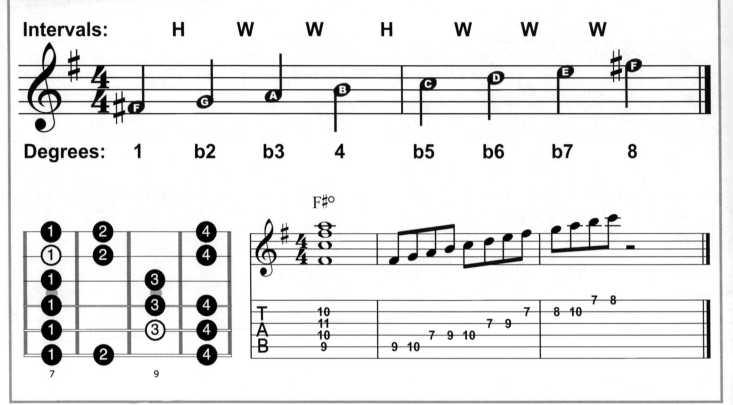

SUNDAY: SCALE APPLICATION

Today's example illustrates the sound of each mode by playing the triad built from each scale degree, literally outlining each mode's strongest notes. For further study, you can turn each of the CAGED positions into each of the modes. The scale fingerings will remain the same.

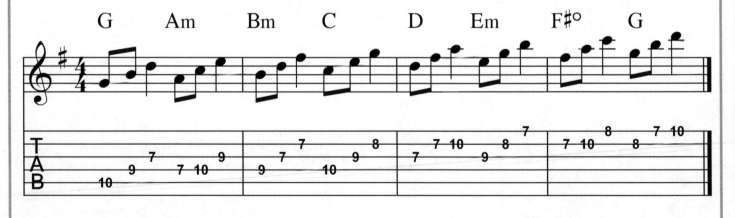

MONDAY: "B♭ BLUES"

Our final example is a B♭ jazz blues that employs a variety of scales we've learned, including major and minor pentatonic, the Mixolydian mode, harmonic minor, and the blues scale.

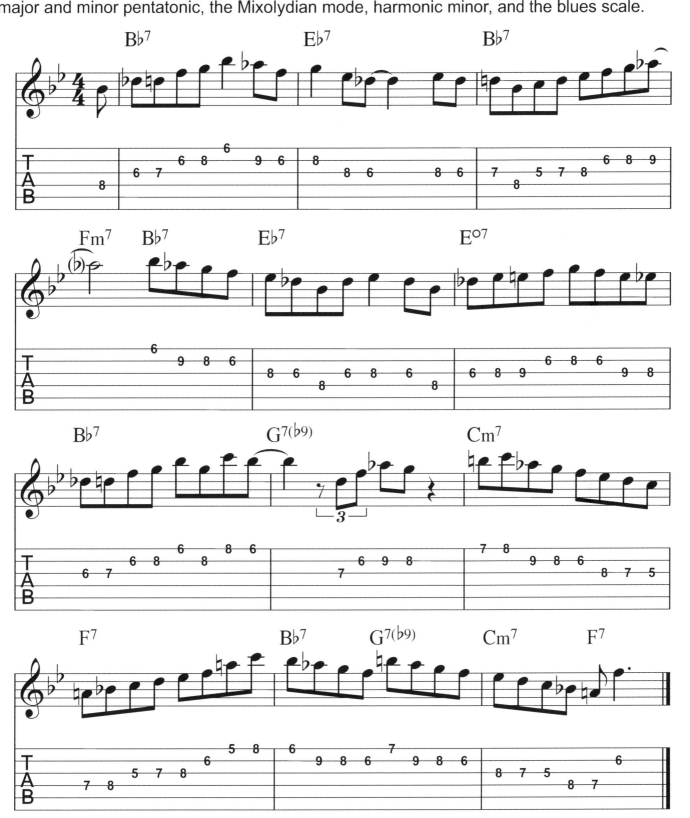

ABOUT THE AUTHOR

Since he was just three years old, Milwaukee-area guitarist **Kirk Tatnall** has been chasing music via his favorite vehicle: the guitar. In addition to authoring instructional books, Kirk continues to perform, compose, record, and release original music, teach guitar, and lend his playing to other artists and various commercial music sessions. For more details, please visit his website: *kirktatnall.com*.

Made in the USA
Columbia, SC
29 December 2024

50814756R00093